THE BUSINESS SCALING BLUEPRINT

TONY DISILVESTRO

THE BUSINESS SCALING

BLUEPRINT

Building a Foundation to Grow Your Brand

Forbes | Books

Published by Forbes Books, Charleston, South Carolina.
Member of Advantage Media.

Forbes Books is a registered trademark, and the Forbes Books colophon is a trademark of Forbes Media, LLC.

Printed in the United States of America.

10 9 8 7 6 5 4 3 2 1

ISBN: 978-1-95588-449-5 (Hardcover)
ISBN: 979-8-88750-004-1 (eBook)

LCCN: 2022916514

Cover design by Amanda Haskin.
Layout design by Analisa Smith.

This custom publication is intended to provide accurate information and the opinions of the author in regard to the subject matter covered. It is sold with the understanding that the publisher, Forbes Books, is not engaged in rendering legal, financial, or professional services of any kind. If legal advice or other expert assistance is required, the reader is advised to seek the services of a competent professional.

Since 1917, Forbes has remained steadfast in its mission to serve as the defining voice of entrepreneurial capitalism. Forbes Books, launched in 2016 through a partnership with Advantage Media, furthers that aim by helping business and thought leaders bring their stories, passion, and knowledge to the forefront in custom books. Opinions expressed by Forbes Books authors are their own. To be considered for publication, please visit **books.Forbes.com**.

For my grandfather, Bucky. Your belief in me thirty years ago is why I am successful today. And for my wife, Cyndi. Thanks for supporting me no matter how many crazy ideas I had.

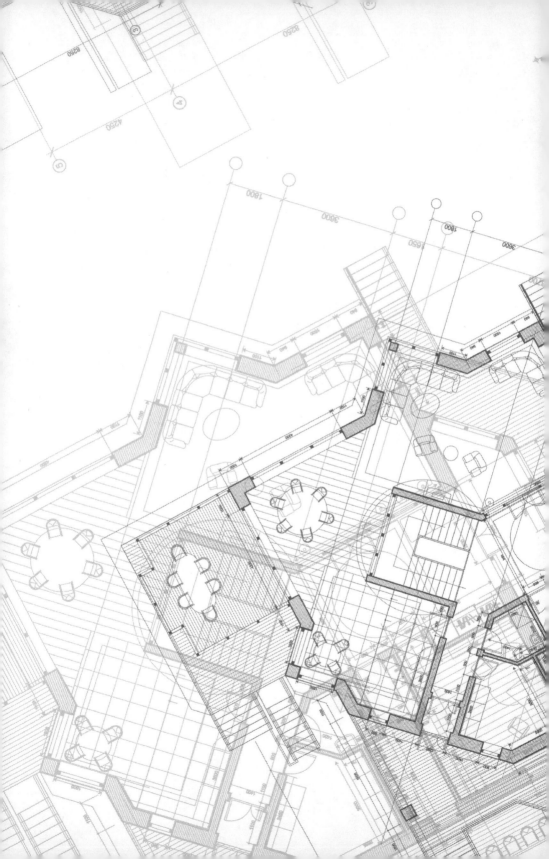

CONTENTS

PREFACE

HOW TO USE THIS BOOK

Over the years, I've coached hundreds of entrepreneurs and business owners who have big dreams and ambitions. And I've come to notice that there is one main trait that separates those who succeed from those who struggle. The winners take action. Yes, you need a good idea. You need to have a brand and know your customer and market your business. You need those things, and you'll find out how to achieve them in the pages of this book. But I'd argue that those are not the biggest predictors of success. Action-taking is. Those who take action succeed. They might fail faster, but they learn faster. They course correct as they're already in motion. They go for it. They don't wait until everything is perfect. They fix things as they go.

That's what I want you to do, and I want you to use this book as your guide. Write all over it, fold over the pages, drip your morning coffee on it. Rip out the pages and tape them on your wall if you want to! What I don't want you to do is read half of it and then put it on the shelf. When you read a chapter, stop and implement the material.

Don't move on until you're ready. Reread if you want to. But please just take some action and make some moves. That's my hope for you and the main goal for this book. I want to inspire you to get off your butt and get in the game.

You'll hear a lot of my story throughout this book. I've achieved a lot, and I still have big dreams I'm working toward. I'm a serial entrepreneur who can't sit still and who is always growing, improving, and looking forward. But I never had a huge advantage in life. My parents weren't rich, and I grew up working my entire life. Until I started my own business, I worked at gas stations and pizza parlors. I didn't go to a fancy school or have a fancy mentor.

> **Trying things, failing, trying again, succeeding, and continuing to move forward. If there's a silver bullet to success, it's that.**

What I had was guts and a little entrepreneurial blood. I had a risk-taking mindset and the confidence that I could make it work—perhaps too much at times. I gained a lot of wisdom along the way, which you'll find in these pages. But none of this would have happened if I didn't keep taking action. Trying things, failing, trying again, succeeding, and continuing to move forward. If there's a silver bullet to success, it's that.

I hope you use this book as your constant companion. Don't be precious with it; rough it up and absorb the information. And then get out there and make stuff happen! I'm honored to be on this journey with you. If I can do it, you can do it. You just have to get out there and try. Let's get to it!

Stop Working in Your Business and Start Working on It

BUSINESS OWNERS OWN A JOB; ENTREPRENEURS OWN A VISION.

Four months of hurry and eight months of worry. That was my family's motto growing up on the Jersey Shore. I was born into an entrepreneurial family. My dad worked three jobs to provide for our family. He was a milkman, a police officer, and a construction worker, and he owned some rental properties. My mom had a macrame business. Living in a touristy area, we knew we had to work hard to make up for the lull during the winter months. My two siblings and I contributed a lot and inherited my parents' work ethic. We had a big, warm, loving Italian family, but my parents ran a tight ship, too.

I officially started my first business at eight years old. I went down to the wholesale candy store and bought a bunch of bubble gum and candy bars. Then I set up a table on the oceanfront and sold them as people were coming off the beach. At nine years old, I was already hungry to create my own thing. I began helping my mom sell Mexican pottery in her macrame shop. I worked sixty hours and sold hundreds of pots a week. I genuinely loved it. Customer service was in my blood. Even at such a young age, it didn't feel like work. It was thrilling. I felt important, and I knew I was helping my family. My next business venture was selling fruits and vegetables on the back of a pickup truck at all the resort hotels. And on and on the business ventures went. I pumped gas, changed oil, made pizzas, etc. I couldn't stop thinking about creating businesses and seeing opportunities all around me. I was blessed to learn the value of a customer at such an early age. My dad once handed me a five-dollar bill and said, "Flip it over." I did. It read, "In God We Trust." "No," he said. "*That's* the only thing you can trust. Go make a bunch of those." And so I did.

I made my first pizza when I was fifteen. I was working at a gas station at the time, and the owner came in one day and said, "Kid, come here. You're going to learn to make pizza today." He also owned a pizzeria, and his pizza guy had just quit. That day changed my life, and very soon I knew I eventually wanted to own my own restaurant. It made sense and combined all the things I loved: family, food, and selling. I continued working in restaurants, moved up to the Manhattan area for a while, went to college, and eventually was ready to open my own pizzeria.

I did some research and decided Virginia Beach was where I would open my restaurant. At twenty-one, I jumped in the car with my girlfriend, who later became my wife, and we moved down south. But opening a business is expensive, and you often need capital or a loan, and no one would give me one. My parents weren't in a position to help, either. So I went to my step-grandfather, Bucky, who was also an entrepreneur and believed in my vision. He wrote me a $60,000 check. I was enormously grateful, but even thirty years ago, that was barely enough to open a restaurant. I had already decided where I wanted our first location to be, but I kept hitting roadblocks. The landlord told me over and over that nothing was available, so I took a job at another pizzeria and waited. I would not compromise on location, as I just knew this was it. Two years later, the location opened up, and I signed a lease. Even though we barely had enough money, we made it work, and in 1993 I opened the first Ynot Pizza. Ynot is Tony spelled backward, and it is also a childhood nickname that was given to me because it embodies my entire outlook on life: "Why not?" I got so comfortable selling and growing a business in front of strangers at such a young age that it helped me develop this mindset. I was allowed to do that sort of thing back then, something I know likely wouldn't happen today. There are a lot of reasons for my success, but this early entry into entrepreneurship is definitely one of them.

Two months after opening, we were in trouble. We were already drastically underfunded when our air conditioner broke, and we spent the last of what we had to fix it. I thought we were going to have to close. But I learned from a young age that quitting was never an option, so I found a way forward. I talked to one of my food distributors, who floated me a $12,000 loan to keep going. Six months later, we had another loss, and the future of the company was in jeopardy again. And again we kept going. I have had plenty of losses and failures that I'll share with you throughout this book, and each one has made me stronger and smarter. They made me better and taught me lessons that I now teach to others.

Within a year, Ynot took off, and I was able to pay back both of my loans. Now it's a booming business with seven franchises. It's also a family affair, as my three daughters and my brother work with us. And Ynot is only one of many businesses I have started. I have founded more than thirty-one businesses with over 450 employees in a variety of industries, including real estate, construction, restaurants, commercial buildings, manufacturing, and SaaS. Looking back on those early days, I was so fortunate to have been born in that small Jersey town where I learned how to communicate with customers at such a young age. Even today, many years, over thirty businesses, and a few million dollars later, I tell my coaching clients that we're all in the same business: the people business. Whether it's employees to hire or customers to sell to, it takes 98.6 degrees to accomplish your goals.

All of this experience has led me here, to write this book and share these ideas. In addition to running my businesses, I'm now a coach and mentor. Running a business is hard. Those early days can be rough. I worked over a hundred hours a week for years. I missed the first five years with my oldest daughter. I ran myself ragged, and it affected everything about my life. I also wanted to grow and soon learned that I couldn't do it like that. Something had to give. But I didn't have a mentor. I didn't have anyone coaching me or teaching me how to market, delegate, train, and scale my business. I had to figure all of that out on my own. And now the most important thing I do is to be the coach for others that I never had.

All of us get into business because we are passionate about something, right? You have a great skill and want to use it to help people. You're what I call a technician. And then you get started and decide you have to do everything. Maybe you think you're the only one who can do it right or you don't have the money to hire help or you don't have good systems in place. Either way, you feel stuck. You figure the harder you work, the more successful you'll be. But you try that and it still doesn't move the needle. You want to grow, but you aren't. It's because you're a business owner, not an entrepreneur. You're working *in* your business, not *on* your business. I see this all the time, and it's the biggest obstacle to scaling. If you want to grow and start making the impact you were born to make, you need to stop being a business owner and start thinking like an entrepreneur. When I got started, I thought I was the only one who could make pizzas, as I was the fastest pizza maker in the world in 1994. Nobody told me to get out of the kitchen and look at the bigger picture. It wasn't until many years later, when an injury forced me out, that I realized I was the bottleneck and that the business couldn't grow unless I started doing things differently.

According to the US Bureau of Labor Statistics, in the first two years of operation, 20 percent of businesses in America fail. In the first five years, that number jumps to 45 percent. Fewer than 25 percent of businesses make it beyond fifteen years. It's even harder in the restaurant business. In my opinion, the closing of even a single business is painful. It's excruciating for me to see people go out of business. It's a broken dream, with countless hours of work and expectations down the drain. There are even economic implications. Our economy is run by small- to medium-sized businesses. There is a lot at stake, and I feel the intensity of it every single time I see a business shut down. I have lost two substantial businesses in the past, and my purpose in life is to help entrepreneurs win. My passion is to reduce the amount of failing business around the world.

Entrepreneurial resilience is crucial.

The purpose of this book, as well as my coaching practice, is to prevent that from happening. Compromising your dream is a recipe for depression and living in regret. Your passion and fulfillment are worth fighting for. People who start a business often give up too easily. They start with passion, but the fire burns out because of the stress and demands. It's not because they didn't try hard enough; it's because they didn't have the right guidance. They didn't know what their brand stands for or how to market, delegate, systemize, and scale. That's what you'll learn here. I have helped hundreds of others with these very simple yet important principles. Most entrepreneurs who quit likely didn't have the mindset necessary to withstand the inevitable trials of building a business. Entrepreneurial resilience is crucial. You can have all the tools you need, but if your mind isn't in the right place, you won't make it. I'll repeat it multiple times throughout this book, so you better get used to it: this is all about mindset.

I'm not a pie-in-the-sky fancy businessman talking to you from a pedestal. I'm down in the trenches, practicing everything I preach all day long. I'm a mentor and a coach. Every principle in this book is learned from hard-won wisdom and is implemented in every one of my businesses every day. I didn't just do this stuff twenty years ago. I did it yesterday, I did it today, and I'll do it tomorrow. Entrepreneurship has always been a way of life for me. I have always seen life as an exciting adventure; it's a fun game with opportunities everywhere. Meeting people's needs, creating amazing experiences for them—there's just nothing better than that. It's what makes me tick. It's why I get out of bed every morning. If you're a new business owner or the CEO, this book will help you get it right from the start and lay a good foundation while helping you avoid many of the mistakes I made. If you're in the thick of it and struggling to stay afloat, this book will help you course correct and make some changes to get your life back and run your business more efficiently. And if you're ready, you can start scaling your business however big you want it to go. The sky is the limit. First, we have to figure out your why. Or your *Y* as I like to call it. It's the *Y* in Ynot. It's the foundation of your brand and the entire business. I'm honored to be your coach and to watch you scale to new heights. You can create the business and life of your dreams. We can do it together. Let's create an experience.

The Three Pillars

A DEFINED PATH INSPIRES.

In business, experience is gold. It is more valuable than mechanical or technical skills. Wisdom is precious currency. One wise decision can save you hours and huge amounts of dollars. In the early years of business, if I had known what I know now, I could have avoided a lot of mistakes. Instead of mistakes, let's call them opportunities for growth. I like to keep things positive. I don't regret a single day of my life, because if I didn't have both the losses and the wins, I would not be who I am today.

A few years into the success of Ynot, many people asked me how we'd been so prosperous, especially in the cutthroat restaurant business. I had beaten the entrepreneurial odds, and Ynot was ahead of the game. I wasn't a mentor yet, but people were starting to ask me about my success. I was also getting frustrated with our employees because I had created an awesome mission statement that was a few sentences long, but when I walked around our restaurants talking to team members, no one knew what it was. Some people had worked for me for years and still couldn't recite the mission statement! I was annoyed. So I sat down that day to think this problem through.

What came out of me was a tool that has been nothing short of amazing for my business and for hundreds of others that I have worked with. It streamlined my vision and every process in my brand. And best of all, it's easy for my team members to remember, and it gave them a clear vision, too. The system is the three pillars.

THREE SIMPLE WORDS, ONE BIG PURPOSE

The three pillars are three words. They are the Y—the personality and the vision of your brand. The three pillars will become the foundation of every aspect in your brand. They will help you define your training programs, how you hire, how you delegate, and how you develop focused marketing campaigns. The three pillars will develop the founder's or CEO's vision and make sure it resonates with the customer. When I start working with companies, this is my first step, because from here I create the foundation to scale any business. This process can be daunting, but I promise that if you put the work in, it will pay off in huge dividends. The three pillars encompass everything. They become the lens through which you see everything in your business and through which every decision is made. You think about them when you hire, market, train, and delegate. They are not just the mission of the managers and owners but of everyone, customers and employees alike. Everyone has to feel them, know them, and embody them. I am fanatical about this. If people don't get this part right, nothing else will work. It is worth thinking through deeply and spending a lot of time to figure it out. It's the first thing I always do when I speak publicly and coach entrepreneurs privately. It always starts with the three pillars.

The three pillars of Ynot Italian are **FAMILY, QUALITY**, and **COMMUNITY**.

This is the Ynot way. We are so dedicated to this that if you walk into any Ynot restaurant, you'll notice that everything from the decor to the food is the product of these three pillars. Let's look at the family aspect first to help explain this concept.

We are the restaurant where people come to create memories that span a lifetime. When I first sat down and wrote out the Y behind my business, my vision included everyone from children to grandparents. When I built my first restaurant, I tiled the floors, added high chairs, and designed kids' coloring books. My vision was to create a neighborhood restaurant where families felt welcome. On the first day, I noticed that everybody who came in was there with family. I always wanted to open a family restaurant, and initially I thought people would come to the counter and order like they do at Panera. But when the first customer came in, they sat down right away. They asked if a server was coming over. *Of course!* I thought. *People are coming here to sit down and break bread together. They want to enjoy a meal, laugh, and look each other in the eye.* The pillar of family in my business came very quickly and naturally. I'm Italian, so everything I ever did was always about family. When I was young, if you walked into my grandma's house and didn't give her a kiss right away, you were dead. I grew up having big, loud, loving family gatherings around meals. And now I share all of those traditions with my three daughters. It was only natural for this to become the foundation of my business.

This pillar filters down and affects every part of my business. We're family-friendly. We use tiles everywhere so that if kids come in, they can spill drinks, stomp on food, and do what they like, and it will be quick and easy to clean up. But it's about a lot more than that. Family is a mindset perspective. We are mindful of everything we do so that we treat our customers and employees like family. We have customers who started coming as kids and still visit when they're back in town from college. When I hire employees, I have legacy on my mind. I want my staff to be so satisfied with their work environment that they would want their family members to come work for us. I don't believe in just managing my employees but coaching them into becoming whatever they want to be. I take a personal interest in their lives and their professional goals for growth. I sit with them and map out plans. I make sure that work is engaging enough to keep them interested and fulfilled. We have had many employees whose children come work for us when they're old enough. This makes me incredibly happy. Sustainability in a business is not just about cash flow or growth; it is about relationships. It's about keeping people happy and holding on to those who really matter. It's about family.

> **Sustainability in a business is not just about cash flow or growth; it is about relationships.**

DEFINE YOUR BRAND

So what is your brand? Do you have any idea yet? It's okay if you don't. Let's talk through it. Here's a helpful exercise. Write down three words that you believe represent your brand. What does your brand stand for? What are you known for? What do your customers perceive? What do your employees think of the brand? Brainstorm and write down three words. Even if you don't feel they are perfect, you need to start somewhere. Now, underneath each word, write ten more words that mean approximately the same thing. Here's an example from my construction business, Ynot Build.

INTEGRITY	QUALITY	EXPERIENCE
Honesty	Craftsmanship	Trust
Principle	Excellence	Family
Sincerity	Standards	Tranquility
Virtue	Reliability	Reality
Candor	Value	Involvement
Thoughtfulness	Dependable	Legacy
Honorable	Superior	Exposure
Straightforward	Innovative	Satisfaction
Reputation	Perfection	Success
Ethics	Longevity	Dreams

All of these words are basically synonyms, but they resonate with you differently, right? There are similarities to the words. The purpose of this exercise is to help define why you're doing what you're doing. Why is the customer coming through your front door? We'll get into this more in a later chapter, but everything you do creates an experience. You are an experience creator. What kind of experience are you trying to create for your customers and your employees? The first words you come up with are almost never the words you eventually settle on. This method cannot be rushed; it's a big process. Sometimes it can take weeks or months to land on exactly the right words. It might drive you crazy! You might struggle with it for a long time and then eventually have an epiphany. Good! Stick with it. We're building the foundation here. Remember, this will affect absolutely everything, and I mean everything, in your business and take you to the next level. This process is also helpful because the more specific you can be, the better. These words will become the message you're projecting to the world and will attract the kinds of customers and employees you want to work with. This is how we create experiences every day.

A big part of this process is helping you form your customer avatar. A customer avatar is an industry-specific term that means your ideal customer—the type of person you want to purchase your products or services. As you do this deep dive into your brand and think about the experience you want to create, also think about who you're serving. Are they industry experts? Are they professionals? Are they relaxed and chill or buttoned-up and fancy? Are they young or old? What do they care about? Family became my first pillar largely because family is my customer avatar. I serve families, and I create a unique family experience in my restaurants. My middle daughter has a jewelry business. As she was defining her brand, she had to think through who she was selling to. Do they want Rolexes? Do they like gold or silver? How much money do they have to spend? Why do they wear jewelry? What special occasions do they have going on? All of this contributes to the kind of jewelry she carries and how she markets her business. It's all about her customer avatar and the experience she's creating.

Sophie is an all-star coaching client of mine. She has a medical staffing firm located in Texas and Florida that she founded in 2018.

They provide healthcare professionals with placement in urgent care centers, family practices, and hospitals. They even do some placement overseas. She gets a lot of joy out of helping employees find that dream job and workplaces find the perfect fit. I first met Sophie at a speaking event in Florida. She came up to me after my talk, and we clicked instantly. I began coaching her that month.

On our first call, we talked about her three pillars. I'm telling you, this is foundational stuff. It's where I start with everyone. The first pillars she came up with were enthusiastic, agile, and credentials. But after just one call with her, I could tell these were not reflective of her business at all. She hadn't gone nearly deep enough. So I kept asking her and asking her, forcing her to think harder about her brand and the experience she creates for both her customers and her employees. She kept listing words, and we got closer with every call. Next, she chose effectiveness, solution-driven, and agile. Those were better, but we still hadn't thought we nailed it. See how this can take some time? It can be maddening! But it forces you to get deep. This process with Sophie lasted months before we ended up with her final pillars of reactive, customized, and solutions. I spent many hours pulling the vision out of her head. What is different about your company? How are you disrupting the market? Why do you think you're better than your competitors? We never would have come up with these authentic pillars if we first hadn't invested in this process. Here's what they mean to her business.

REACTIVE: Her business name is 24/7 Healthcare Staffing. They answer the phone twenty-four hours a day, seven days a week. Most staffing companies that offer this same service close at 5:00 p.m. But not Sophie. This sets her apart. It's very unique to her brand. By being reactive, her clients know she is the perfect fit, which helps 24/7 Healthcare Staffing differentiate themselves from their competition.

CUSTOMIZE: Sophie finds the exact credentials her clinics and hospitals are looking for in a healthcare professional. Every position is different and looking for unique things in a person. Just because someone is a doctor doesn't mean that they'll be a good fit for this specific clinic or that they'll have the exact experience to serve those patients best. At 24/7 Healthcare Staffing, they examine every aspect of urgent care needs, whether they are looking for a doctor who can get patients in and out or they are concerned about bedside manner. Then Sophie interviews each employee to make sure they are the perfect fit.

SOLUTION: Sophie's clients have an immediate problem and need an immediate solution. Sophie now understands that a problem is an opportunity and that opportunities create solutions. But they don't just need a warm body for that day. They need someone who will meet their long-term needs, and the employee wants a job that they find satisfying and rewarding—or they're just going to be calling Sophie again a week from now with the same problem.

This has changed everything for Sophie, as it should! It changed the way she talks about her business and markets it to clients. It changed the things she focuses on day-to-day, and it's dramatically changed her cash flow. Now she is confident with her brand promise and is constantly hiring, scaling, and signing huge contracts. I am so proud of Sophie. She has worked so hard, and it's easy when someone wants to be coached and puts in the hard work. That's the power of these exercises.

GET THE TEAM INVOLVED

If you already have a business, a good way to spark more ideas and to get feedback on what your brand stands for is to ask your customers.

One of the most helpful things to do is to ask them what words come to mind when they think of your business. It can be scary and nerve-racking to open yourself up to this kind of assessment. It makes you feel vulnerable. But that insight into your customer's mind is gold. Even if you've never consciously thought about what your brand stands for, it does stand for something. When you create a business, you create a brand, whether you do it on purpose or not. This is the point here: to do it on purpose. Remember what we touched on before: You got into this because you are great at something. You're a technician. But what does your business really stand for? Have you ever stopped to think about it? So many of my coaching clients have never done this simple exercise and believe that their business just stands for "being good at X." Whether you are a small business or a CEO at a large company, your employees and customers need to understand your vision and mission. The three pillars will help you articulate your mindset and develop a clear mission statement.

If you think you've nailed your three pillars, here's the real test. Go ask your employees what they think they are. That's a real gut check. If you think your business is all about integrity, but that word (or one like it) never comes up when you ask your employees, something is off and you need to figure out where. They will truly reflect back to you what your business is all about. It can either be enlightening and teach you something valuable about your business that you want to keep doing, or it might show you a misalignment in your vision and the experience that is actually being created for the customer. Be open to hearing this feedback, even if it's hard, as you may need to recalibrate your marketing or training.

The three pillars start with you, but the real magic happens when you get your employees to buy into them as well. I mentioned before that none of my team members could remember our mission statement. I have found this to be true at every business I've been to. I often ask the owners if they can recite their mission statements and 75 percent usually can't. And almost 99 percent of employees can't recite it at all. What good is it if your employees don't know what your brand stands for? The three pillars are your mission statement. Getting your team members to understand your three pillars is where the real power lies in this process. When your staff fully understands what they're doing and why, that's when you can create a real experience for your customer. Your staff are the true experience creators. They cannot execute on your vision and mission if you aren't teaching them what the company stands for and the Y behind everything they do. If you're still stuck on what your three pillars are, keep asking your employees and your customers until you nail it. Ask them what they think your company stands for. Ask them what three words they would use to describe the brand. What do they feel when they come to work? Just like your customers, getting into their minds can generate invaluable feedback.

People want to be part of something bigger than themselves. Some people just want a job, but most people want something more, especially the younger generation. Clarifying your three pillars will attract the kind of people who will help you scale and further your mission. These factors greatly affect how I hire people. I always want to know if they value being part of a family. Is that important to them? What do they do in the community? How do they present themselves? Without the three pillars guiding me, I have no idea what I'm looking for, and I'll end up with all the wrong people. Another fantastic aspect of this idea is that these words can mean different things to different people, but they are no less impactful. When I asked my team members what family meant to them, I got a lot of different answers. One said, "Getting two weeks off when my mom was diagnosed with cancer." Another said, "My son working here twenty years after I did." Some people have a complicated view of their biological family, so it means something entirely different. That's the beauty of the three pillars and not pigeonholing everyone into a specific mission statement. Your staff has to be invested in the pillars, but this allows for their own personal interpretation. As I've said, we're in the people business, and people are complicated. You need to guide and instruct them while allowing for their humanity.

DIG A LITTLE DEEPER

Let's expand on the pillar of quality. Quality is everything to me. I have a construction company called Ynot Build. The three pillars of that company are integrity, quality, and experience, like the example I used earlier. In construction, quality doesn't just mean I'm building a quality home. That's obvious. It means I'm using quality products, quality two-by-fours, quality paint, and even quality doorknobs. It applies to the workers I hire. If I hire a subcontractor who doesn't do quality work or comes to work with their shirt untucked or doesn't pick up after their crew, I can't say I'm a quality builder. I have a framer who I trust and use all the time. Every time he walks into a job, he says hi to everyone and is very polite and friendly; he makes people feel comfortable. When he leaves, the place is immaculate. He understands that he's working on people's dreams, and he acts like it. At the end of the day, I'm creating an experience for my construction clients, and if quality isn't one of my pillars, the chance of them having a great experience with me is low. This is where all three of those pillars intertwine. I have integrity as a builder because my clients can trust the quality of my work and the wonderful experience I create for them.

Notice that community is a pillar for Ynot Italian but not for my construction business. Community might be a pillar for some construction companies if you're building things for a planned community, like a gym or a public space, but I build luxury homes. I'm a custom builder specializing in single high-dollar houses. Many times they're on the water or in the back of a neighborhood, and I don't ever think about community. It's a very different business from my restaurants, in the same way that McDonald's would not list quality as one of their pillars. They might say something more like convenience, value, and consistency. They are one of the most successful restaurants in the world, and I don't think they've ever been focused on quality. The three pillars are incredibly unique and specialized, even among businesses that might seem very similar on the surface.

My employees and I have a dress code. We wear polo shirts with the Ynot Italian logo. Sometimes I walk into meetings or coaching sessions covering the *not* in Ynot with my hand so that it just reads Y. Then I ask, "What is your why?" There are a thousand Ys in my business. It's a fun idea that people remember. And if you take a closer look at the letter *Y*, you will see the inspiration for the name of this three pillars tool—it's a three-pronged letter. It's just another visual reminder to always be thinking about those words. I am dogmatic about this, so get used to me talking about it.

One of the most important benefits of the three pillars is the direction they give when you begin to scale. A consistent dynamic is created within your organizational structure that keeps the momentum going. Even in moments of chaos, you don't lose anything, because everyone knows what to do and where we're headed. If you walk into Ynot on a Friday night, you will witness what I call controlled chaos. I have my operational structure down to a science. When the restaurant is bursting with customers, you will walk into a hive buzzing with busy waiters making a beeline from the kitchen to the tables, from the tables to the cash register, from the cash register to another table, etc. To an observer, this might look like utter mayhem, but it's all happening in a controlled manner. Occasionally you might hear a crash of utensils or witness a near collision. But all that is expected when work gets busy. In fact, I even plan for mishaps in my budget. It's normal. The place keeps humming along even during the busiest, most stressful times because the three pillars are in place. They have directed all the decisions I made to get us here: the staff I chose, the decor, the menu, the attire, the processes, the systems—everything. They help team members navigate daily tasks and hard situations. They execute the experience. We always maintain our standards because we know what they are. In fact, our busiest nights are the best, because it's showtime! After you've talked through and thought about the three pillars enough, they become instinctual, and your team hardly has to stop and think. They just know what to do. Everyone has a clear vision, and you're able to create the best experience possible.

Before we end this chapter, I have to address naming your company. I have changed the name of so many of my clients' businesses that I can't even keep track anymore. One of my favorite clients, who will come up again throughout this book, has a surfboard shop. His name is Nick. The original name of Nick's shop was Dirtbag Surf Co. Kinda catchy, right? Certainly memorable. But the problem is, Nick's unique selling proposition is that he makes the surfboards in-house with his customers, and it's a family affair. He primarily markets to kids and parents who come in and make surfboards together as a fun bonding activity. Does having *dirtbag* in the title conjure up a fun, family-friendly environment? Not at all. And this didn't click for Nick until we got deep into his pillars, and he began applying it in his marketing. More on that later. But the point here is that if drilling down on your three pillars makes you realize you need a new business name, go ahead and change it. I know that might be scary, but it's important. If you want to scale, you need to adapt. I have changed the name of my restaurant three times because my customer avatar changed.

STOP

Stop. Seriously. Do you have your three pillars down? Don't turn the page until you can honestly say you've done the work here. There are almost no words strong enough to impress on you how important this piece of your business is. When you feel you have nailed your three pillars, your marketing will produce results, your employees will have confidence to execute, and you will create amazing customer experiences. This is everything. You market with it, delegate with it, systemize with it, and scale with it. The pillars are a thread throughout the rest of the principles in this book as well as a lens through which to make every decision. We won't stop talking about the three pillars here. They will come up in every single chapter, and your knowledge and understanding of them will deepen. Once you have your three pillars down, you can stop wasting time, money, and effort. You can read on to all of the other fundamental principles in this book and be able to implement them tenfold because you have a clear vision. You'll be ready to scale and take everything to the next level. But first you need to get honest with yourself: Why are you doing what you're doing? When was the last time you stopped and thought about that? That's where you start. Whether you've been at this so long that you've lost passion for your business or you're just beginning, start here and don't move on until you're 100 percent sure you've nailed your three pillars and they resonate deep within you and everything you do. After you do that, you'll be unstoppable.

⚖ ACTION STEPS

1. Start with three words that you think might be your pillars. Look at those words and then list ten more. Don't be afraid to whip out your thesaurus if you need to. Choose three to start with as your pillars.

2. Answer this question: Why do I do what I do?

3. Answer this question: What kind of experience am I trying to create for my customers?

4. Answer this question: Who is my ideal customer avatar? Who do I serve?

5. Interview customers about your business. Ask them why they buy your products or services. Ask them about their experience with you. What comes to mind when they think of the brand?

6. Interview employees. Ask them what it's like to work for you. Why do they work for you? What comes to mind when they think of the products and services? What is the experience they create for customers?

7. Does your marketing relate to your three pillars?

8. Do your employees understand your Y?

Again, *stop*. Don't move on until you fully understand this part. Reread the chapter if you have to. Do the work. Then move on. Let's do it.

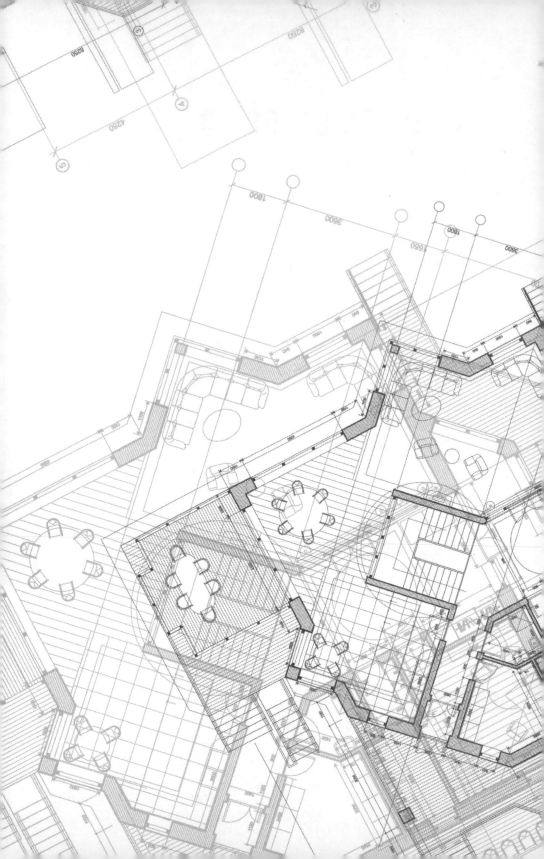

CHAPTER 2

Systemize to Grow

LEARN EVERY DAY OR DIE.

Many years ago, after the success of my first restaurant, I wanted to open a second one. *I can just open another restaurant,* I thought. *We're successful. It's going to be easy.* Just like that, we opened another restaurant on a college campus. I thought it was a no-brainer—I have a quality brand with amazing food. My other restaurant had only been open for two years and already we had a second location. I was crushing it! But very soon after opening, things weren't going so well. Nobody was following my policies. The staff weren't following procedures. Customers were not coming in. It didn't make sense. The restaurant was a mess, orders were getting botched, and it just seemed like nothing was working. I didn't understand. I had done this once before and done it really well. My other restaurant was running great! I had even gotten to a point where I thought it wasn't so hard anymore and wondered what everybody's problem was. This should be easy. Why wasn't it working like the other restaurant?

The restaurant was struggling so much. I was over $200,000 in debt and had lost over $600,000. We eventually had to pull the plug. I was only twenty-six. It turned out that it wasn't anybody's problem but my own. I hadn't taken any of those thought processes and whys behind everything we did at the first location and put them on paper. I hadn't documented anything—no systems, processes, or procedures. In short, I hadn't systemized anything. Nobody knew what to do because I hadn't created replicable systems for others to follow. Well, perhaps I had, but they existed only in my head, which doesn't count for much. I also didn't understand my customer avatar: the kids on campus couldn't afford my restaurant.

So I started with job descriptions and standard operating procedures. I began the tedious process of writing down every single thing every person in the restaurant does. Over the course of the next few years, my systems were improving. But the hard truth was that it still wasn't great. I had to keep revisiting our systems over and over, getting more granular every time. I rewrote the documents again and again, each time focusing on every individual and every problem they might encounter. "This is how we close the restaurant store every night, take the same exact path, etc." And eventually my new restaurants became well-oiled machines, though if you're continually growing, the work of systemizing is never done because things could always improve, even if just by 1 percent. Even after thirty years, I'm always looking for friction points so that I can create solutions every day.

Systems create consistency, and consistency is key to scaling and entrepreneurship.

This chapter is all about systemizing your processes and turning them into systems. Processes can be loose and haphazard, but systems are replicable and sustainable. It's about looking at every single detail, every single process, and documenting it. This is fundamental to growth. Systems create consistency, and consistency is key to scaling and entrepreneurship. Whether it's my wind turbine business or my SaaS company, consistency is how you deliver results every time, no matter who is performing a task. It's how you create and meet expectations. And, ultimately, like everything I talk about, it's about creating the exact same high-quality customer experience that you're looking to develop, every single time, meeting and exceeding their expectations.

The biggest barrier to systemizing your systems is getting into the technician mindset that I mentioned in the introduction. You started a business because you are great at something or wanted to create a product, but you didn't necessarily think about systems and processes much, right? It's the passion you have for your business that got you started. Maybe, like most of us, you fumbled your way through and figured it out as you went along. When you hired people, you might not have trained them much or just hoped they got it. Most people are still functioning as business owners here and not thinking like entrepreneurs by focusing on this long-term aspect. But at some point, you need to document what you're doing and why in order to grow. Maybe you'll need to hire others and transfer your knowledge to them, or perhaps you just need to get faster and more efficient yourself. Regardless, you cannot grow without systems. You won't scale without them.

When I tell people I'm a contractor, they ask, "How can you build homes? You're a pizza guy." What they don't get is that it's not about the type of business; it's about systemizing your systems. In every business I own, this is where the magic starts. When I'm building one of my concrete homes, I start with an architectural plan, a structural design. It's incredibly difficult to build anything without direction, especially a house. And I have over sixty subcontractors on every job. Everyone is essential and needs to work with others in a specific way at a specific time. The system of this construction is so critically important because if I make one mistake, it might mean having to core drill an entire eleven-inch-thick concrete wall. There's no going back; it's concrete. I can't make that mistake. My project manager is always remarking about how detailed I am on all of my construction jobs, and it's because every process builds on the next, so you need to be thinking three steps ahead. I have to make sure I'm ahead of everybody on the job so that the system doesn't break down. Your business might not involve concrete or multimillion-dollar homes, but the lesson here is the same. Systemizing everything you do up front can save you hours and hours of time and hundreds of thousands to millions of dollars. If you're just starting out in business, begin documenting your processes now. There's no better time. Or if you're an established business or a CEO at a large company and want to grow and create change, look for the friction and develop systems to win. This mindset has given me the ability to scale multiple businesses.

THE THREE PILLARS

Had enough of this yet? Hopefully not, my friend, because it always comes back to the three pillars. Like everything else, when you're systemizing, we start there. When you begin building out your systems, ask yourself with every single step, "Does this align with the three pillars of my brand?" I've refined systems very recently in my business just because I realized that something was out of alignment with my experience pillar, and I completely changed things up so that it would make a bigger impact and a better experience for the customer. In my construction company, I started a quarterly progress inspection with the customer, which created a higher level of communication. This has given my customers comfort and confidence that they hired the right person for the job. After owning my restaurants for almost thirty years, I recently switched to dynamic pricing. These are small changes that resulted in a much bigger impact and a better experience for the customer. Changing means you're growing. This is the granular piece of your brand promise; it's the execution.

To stick with a construction analogy, it's almost like going underneath the three pillars and building the concrete footers that support them. You need to make sure that they are as strong as hell and that the pillars are supported, or else they'll come tumbling down. The pillars are fairly forward facing, and they should be evident to the employee and the client. The processes are the support system to the pillars, making them strong and sturdy so that they stand the test of time. If I'm adding four floors to my building or opening four more stores, I need to make sure my three pillars are in line with my growth plan and my staff. Like the matrix controlling everything behind the beautiful world above. And like Neo and his gang, only you can see it and know how essential it is. Our goal is to be in business for a long time, right? All of this is to sustain your long-term goal of exponential success and growth.

THE THREE STEPS

You already have a system, whether you created one on purpose or not. Just like you already have a brand, whether you thought it through deeply or not. Again, systemizing starts with the pillars, like everything else. The how is fairly straightforward and breaks down into the three steps discussed next. As always, we start with you.

STEP 1: WRITE EVERYTHING DOWN

Write down everything you do all day long. It might take a while. You will likely start out writing fairly high-level things, but keep getting more and more granular. I'm in the process of doing this with my daughter and her jewelry shop. She's now earning multiple six figures with her business and has been doing almost all of it herself. She's finally at a point where she needs to hire more help (which we'll get into later in delegation and training), but first she needs to create systems. She's writing down everything she does all day long so that she can begin passing off many of those tasks and start to scale. That might start out looking like this: write emails, order supplies, post on social media, and make a call to a vendor. That's a good start, but it's not nearly deep enough. She could create email templates to use. Develop a list of common questions and their answers. Document exactly where she buys supplies from, how much, and how to decide what she needs. She could create scripts for interacting on social media and with contracts. This is where true scaling happens. You are creating processes so that you can delegate. Push deeper and deeper into the process. Everyone needs to be able to step into that task and do it well. Systems only work if your employees execute the Y. The three pillars will define your systems.

STEP 2: INVOLVE THE TEAM

If you have employees, a great way to do this is to have your best employee write down their entire day. Take a look at that list, analyze whether you have a successful system for each task, and ask if there is something they would improve. I learn so much from my lower-level employees. I'll also ask another employee in the same position to do the same thing and compare tasks. Are they getting the same results? If their responses are very different, why is that? The answer is almost always because the system is not defined well enough. The more details you define in each task, the better it will resonate across many employees. They all need to be doing the task the same way so that we can create the same experience for the customer.

STEP 3: KEEP PERFECTING, KEEP GROWING

If you haven't figured it out yet, this book is all about mindset and growth. When it comes to systemizing your systems, the work is never done. It's an iterative process and is never finished. Are you open to change? Are you able to adapt? So many people go wrong simply because they are unwilling to change their systems to grow. They come to me and ask, "Why am I not growing?" And the answer is always defining your three pillars and then creating systems that produce the expected result. You have to make sure the systems you have in place are effective. You have to change your processes and procedures every time you experience substantial growth. The processes that got you to $1 million won't get you to $3 million, and those won't get you to $10 million. Or if you're at more of a beginner stage, the processes that got you to $1,000 won't be the same ones to get you to $100,000.

This is crucial to scaling any business, large or small. And when your systems change and your mindset shifts, you have to make sure that translates to your employees and to your management. The whole system must change if you want to grow. When I say systemize your system, I mean at any given point along the way, not just at the beginning. Right now I'm working on a survey to send out to my four hundred employees that asks them, if they were the owner of this company, what would they change? Constantly, every day, even though I have a successful business, I'm looking to improve. Those four hundred minds are more intelligent than me! They look at things differently. I'd be a fool not to ask for their advice. Sometimes we get jaded as the owner or CEO. You start to believe that your way is the best way. This is dangerous. It means you've stopped learning and improving. You need humility in this process. Egos have no place here.

A THOUSAND "Ys"

Every company has a thousand Ys. What I mean is that there needs to be a why behind every process in your business. Because you don't just need to know them; you need to train them and communicate them to your people. One of my coaching clients, Mary, is a real estate agent. I asked her what percentage of listings she ends up landing if she meets with a client. She told me she closes 99 percent of her listings. That's great! She's fantastic at her job. Her business is doing about $3 million a year, and her goal is to get to $10 million. I asked her what that percentage is for the other agents who work for her. She said it was closer to 60 percent. That's a lot less. "I don't really care if you close ninety-nine percent of your listings," I told her. "That discrepancy just tells me that you don't have a system. You have a process that you do well as the owner, but you haven't created a system for your staff to follow and succeed." She needed to communicate her system and the why behind it to her staff.

One of the worst things a customer can say to an owner is, "I only want John or Frank to do my service." That just tells me you don't have a good system. Some of my employees understand why we do things and some really don't. It takes 98.6 degrees to scale. Invest in your people, and they will invest in you. As entrepreneurs, CEOs, and executive-level people, it does no good if only we understand the process. We have to break it down into its smallest elements for others.

Not long ago I was mentoring a company called Rob Bertolino Plumbing. He said when he and his guys go into a house to change a garbage disposal, they lay their red blanket down on the floor to protect it. But is every employee doing this every time? Rob and I talked about the Y—obviously, it is to protect the floor. It also has the added benefit of being more comfortable for the plumber. I pointed out to him that this also tells the customer that you care about their house. It adds to the experience for them and creates a professional perception of you in their mind. It gives them confidence that you'll do a good job. Sometimes it's the small Y that differentiates your business. Rob has a thousand Ys for every process in his business. A system is only strong if you can articulate the why and then have every team member execute.

Knowing the why in every system creates confidence in your employees. It empowers them and gives them purpose. No one likes to be told what to do just for the sake of it. It helps them make good decisions when things inevitably go wrong at some point because they know the deeper thinking behind everything they do. It also encourages them to give feedback and help you improve the systems. They're the ones who will know first when something isn't working well, and if they know the Y behind what you're trying to accomplish, they can help solve the problem.

SYSTEMS CREATE POWERFUL EXPERIENCES

Some of the best things I've learned have been from junior employees. They have changed more processes than anyone else in my companies. Developing a system is one thing, but executing it is another. You need people to execute the system you created, to actually develop the experience you're aiming for. And you need to communicate with those people. How many people go into their businesses, unlock their corporate thirty-story building, and actually think about what they notice when they walk in the front door? Did they notice if the rug was crooked or the blinds were dirty? How did the paint look? Are they talking to the people right there who are acting as the face of the company? I'll tell you right now, if you walk into your office building and don't ask the janitor what he's seeing and feeling about the workplace, you're probably missing 40 percent of what goes on in there. It's the employees—the ones doing the hard work of creating those valuable customer experiences—that can make the biggest difference. They see things we don't see and hear things we don't hear.

So many times at the top of our business, as the people in charge, we think only about our own problems and stress. It's easy to forget about the people actually interacting with customers, who are often the most valuable people in our companies. When I talked to John Legere, the CEO of T-Mobile, he once said that whenever he visits stores, he doesn't talk to the manager. He talks to the person at the front counter who gets face time with customers. I do the same thing in my business. I always try to engage with my employees, whether it's the person sweeping my construction site or the dishwasher in my restaurant. They have all the gold that can really take our business to the next level.

This is daily scaling. I don't just evaluate my processes every year but every day. If I can scale and get 1 percent better every day, that's a win that leads to limitless growth. I love change and growth. If it's not changing, go ahead and dig a six-foot hole and put me in it because I'm done. I can't stand it. As an entrepreneur, you can't have a rearview mirror. Don't look backward. Focus on being better than yesterday, every single day.

EVERY PROBLEM IS AN OPPORTUNITY

When I coach people, one of the first concepts I need them to learn is how to view problems. Problems are opportunities. Opportunities create solutions, solutions create results, and results create return on investment (ROI). When you first start a company, or perhaps when you're hired at a company as a CEO and walk through the door on the first day, you likely don't know what the problems are yet. At this point, you're just using your best instincts as well as the processes that you think are right. But as you get more experience and begin hiring other humans, it becomes easier to see where the friction points are when you find yourself frequently saying, "Why are they doing that?" This is when the growth begins, and the problems of the past become the systems of the future.

I like to start with any position in my company and ask them to tell me some of the problems (opportunities) they're having. I once mentored a guy named Mark who owns a used car lot. He needed help with his sales team, as they were not selling enough cars per month. First, I looked at the system they had in place. Did they understand everything about the cars they're selling? Did they have a training system for every car they sell? Who is the customer avatar? We had to identify his opportunities so that we could create solutions. There was an enormous customer experience problem, and we fixed it. We had to create a system around educating and teaching the sales team about the cars they were selling and then aligning the customers' needs and expected experience with each car.

Another one of my coaching clients recently told me that she is bored out of her mind with her business. Well, that's a huge problem! It's the fastest way to kill growth. It's corporate fatigue, and it's a big opportunity and a wake-up call to hire some new blood or to do something in your business to reignite your passion. Because I promise you, if the CEO is feeling bored and uninspired, that is trickling down to everyone else. I've been in business for over twenty-nine years, and even now I tell my management team that we will likely have 140 problems at one of my stores today because we have seventy employees and each of them has two hands. We're dealing with people here; people make mistakes and everyone is different. There will always be opportunities; it's the solution that creates the result.

> **There will always be opportunities; it's the solution that creates the result.**

One of my biggest rules with my team is that they're always allowed to talk to me about problems, but they absolutely better bring a solution, too. Ultimately, every single day when you walk into your business, there's going to be an opportunity to improve as well as a need to create a system around that solution, or it's going to continue to happen. We don't want to keep dealing with the same problems that we did last month. Correcting someone or identifying a friction point that you can eliminate is great, but it doesn't mean much if it's not integrated into a system that everyone else can repeat. The strength of your business will rest on these solid, granular processes that support your entire team and brand. They might not feel like the sexy, exciting parts of business, but I promise that this is what will make your company great.

ARE YOUR SYSTEMS WORKING?

When was the last time you thought about your systems? Have you ever? Whether you're a one-person operation or a company with one thousand employees, this foundational concept could change everything and take you to the next level. Sometimes, when I begin diving into the systems of my coaching clients, we often discover that they don't perfectly align with one of their three pillars. This often means we need to make a tweak in the process, but it can also mean that the business has evolved in a way that requires changing your three pillars. That does happen, and it's normal. Maybe this is a sign that you've outgrown some old ways of thinking.

One goal for many entrepreneurs is franchising, which is all about systems. When I franchise my restaurant, I'm not actually selling a restaurant. I'm selling a system that allows someone to run a successful restaurant. Franchising is the ultimate business for scale. Whether or not that's your goal, it's important to have this same mindset. Back in 2010, I decided to franchise my business, and I put over one thousand hours into documenting my processes and procedures. I created official handbooks and manuals that included everything from site selection to marketing plans. I enjoyed this because I'm a systems guy. You don't need to systemize at this level right away, but if you have big dreams, this may be a great option for you. Franchising is everything I talked about in this chapter but on steroids.

Begin today. Write down your processes. Systemize them. Develop a program that can create replicable results for everyone in that position and for everyone in your company. Light a fire in those on your team and understand how important this is. Do you have a Y for everything that you do? Do your employees know those Ys, and can they articulate them? Like the human being executing them, these systems are living, breathing, and changing. The work is never done. But you can continue to improve every single day. Opportunities are all around you. Change is what life is all about! Now stop and do a gut check about your systems. Don't read any further unless you have fully understood what it is to systemize your systems and to have predictable results with the outcomes you're looking for. Dig into your business and get your hands dirty. You can do this.

⚗ ACTION STEPS

1. Set aside an entire day to write out everything you do all day long. If you have employees, ask them to do the same.

2. Systemize these tasks. Create a document, a series of videos, or some way to communicate this information to someone else.

3. Examine the system again. Can you get even more granular? Can you create any more assets or information that you or your employees need to accomplish these tasks?

4. Ask someone else with no experience to take a look at it. Do they think they could execute it with the same results you have?

5. When you walk into work today, take a minute to look around and really notice things. Is there an opportunity for improvement? What is one thing you could change to make your company 1 percent better?

6. Ask a customer-facing employee how they think your systems are working. These are the most valuable employees you have. Treat them like it.

7. Name one problem that you can use as an opportunity in your business.

8. Is it time to reevaluate your three pillars?

9. Do your current systems create the expected customer experience?

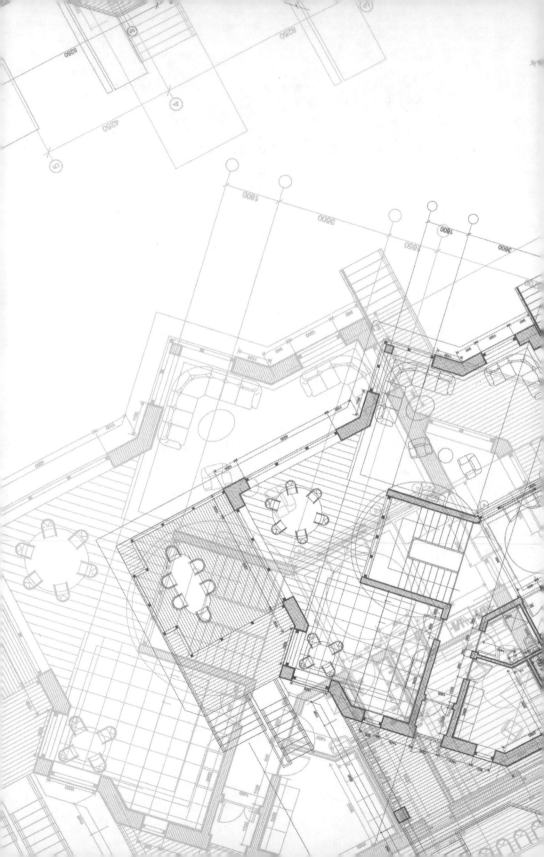

Taking Risks and Failing Well

FAILING WELL DEFINES AN ENTREPRENEUR.

BUSINESS OWNERS, ENTREPRENEURS, AND SERIAL ENTREPRENEURS

When I was making pizzas every day, all day, as a young man in the early days of my business, I thought I was an entrepreneur. I ran my business, still wore my apron all day, and managed to make more pizzas than anyone. But the fact was, I wasn't an entrepreneur at all. I was a business owner. And a stressed out and busy one at that. It wasn't until I was ten years into business that I had a mentor come into my life. His name is Don. Don worked for one of the first marketing companies I worked with. He was about fifteen years older than me and would come in and sit with me and go over business trends. Don and I were very similar; we were growth focused. He used to walk into the store every week and say, "Tony, take that apron off!" But I was stubborn. I believed I could be the best pizza maker and do everything else necessary to run the business. *This is what I do!* I thought. *Hell, it's who I am.* I had been there longer than anybody and could do it all better than everyone else. Not a problem.

But I wasn't growing. Eventually I had to admit that. I had hit a ceiling, and to achieve my growth goals, I had to try something different. The business was entirely dependent on me, and I'm only one person. So one day I finally took his advice, and I took my apron off. I stopped kneading dough and started thinking bigger. A huge part of this was learning to trust the systems I had in place and to begin delegating and trusting my employees to do the work without me (more on this in a later chapter). For years, at least fifty times, Don had given me that advice over and over again, but it wasn't until I had a mindset shift and decided for myself that I could finally take off the apron and scale to the heights I'd dreamed of. Don and I are still close. He came into the store just the other week, and I made sure to tell him, despite how much I fought it at the time, that it was the best advice he'd ever given me. So if you're ready, I'll say the same thing to you: take off the apron.

I want you to hear me loud and clear: Being a business owner is an amazing thing. It's no small feat. There are thousands of people sitting in cubicles in corporate America who dream of being business owners but who never find the courage to try. Being a business owner is an incredible accomplishment. If you own a business, don't take it lightly and wear the term proudly. It's a risk to jump off the cliff and start a business. I give all business owners my utmost respect. They're my favorite people in the world. I used the term *technician* earlier in this book, and I want to expand on that. Many people get into business because they want to work for themselves. Maybe you're a hairdresser and you've worked at a salon for a long time. Everyone tells you what an amazing stylist you are. You're talented, and you're passionate about your work.

Eventually you start to think to yourself, *Maybe I don't need the salon owner or a boss. I'm making my boss so much money, maybe I could just do this for myself. I could open my own salon!* You suggest this to your family, friends, and clients, and they all tell you it's a great idea, or they think you're crazy. They believe in you, which is wonderful. Becoming a business owner is often an emotional decision. You have so much support telling you how great you are. The thought of opening your own salon is exciting and enticing. So you jump in full force and go for it. *I'm the best. I can do it. I'll be better than everyone.* Instantly, you're a technician. This is where 99 percent of us begin.

There's a great documentary on Netflix called *Jiro Dreams of Sushi*. It's about the eighty-five-year-old legendary Japanese sushi chef and owner of Sukiyabashi named Jiro. His restaurant seats only ten people who travel from all over the world and pay top dollar to eat there. It's the only location, and it's earned three Michelin stars. He still makes most of the sushi they serve, and he's done it for the better part of his life. He is an example of the ultimate technician, the ultimate business owner. He doesn't want to scale or grow; he wants to wear the apron. He seems perfectly happy with the size of his business and revenue. More power to him. Could he teach a select few to make sushi as well as he does? Possibly. Could he grow his business and likely make millions of dollars? Almost definitely. But he's a technician and doesn't want to. This is the complete opposite of the way I run my business and the way you need to if you want to grow and scale. This book is about moving from a business owner to an entrepreneur and the mindset that shift requires. This chapter is about the skill set necessary to take that leap and how to know when you're ready.

There are three main categories of people we're going to discuss: business owners, entrepreneurs, and serial entrepreneurs. We've already covered business owners, so let me introduce you to the concept of serial entrepreneurs. I know it well because I am one. It's in my blood, and I've known it all my life. However, while it now works for me in business and is one of the main reasons I'm so successful, in the beginning it was why I made so many mistakes. Business owners who haven't yet jumped into entrepreneurship are usually risk-averse and overly cautious. Innately serial entrepreneurs are the exact opposite. As a young entrepreneur, wisdom didn't come easily to me. I was a crazy risk-taker. I didn't think things through thoroughly. I joined MLM and sold vitamins and opened a photography studio. Looking back, I can't believe I used to do that, considering what I do now. But I was so hungry to get out there and be an entrepreneur! To me, being a serial entrepreneur feels like being chased by a tiger toward a cliff. You have to jump into the water to survive. That's how I felt growing up and working one hundred hours a week for four months of the year from the time I was ten years old. It was jump or die. It's that simple. I had to keep creating and growing because I was being chased by a tiger. That has always stayed with me.

I would argue that taking action is almost always better than taking no action at all, which can keep you stuck for years or perhaps be the reason why you never begin in the first place. But if it's possible, I often took *too much* action. After many, many years of experience, serial entrepreneurs are powerful people. A serial entrepreneurial mindset combined with years of hard-won wisdom is how you create the biggest businesses in the world. But at the beginning, that recklessness can be problematic. I was always growth focused. If there was an opportunity, I would jump in with both feet.

Let's end this discussion on entrepreneurs because that's what I believe most of you are aiming for. Entrepreneurs are right in the middle between the technical, risk-averse business owner and the possibly reckless, action-oriented serial entrepreneur. Entrepreneurs want to scale and grow. They know their business cannot depend solely on them. The main thing I wish I'd had back in my early days is a coach. I suffered so many losses in the first years of business that I bet could have been cut by at least 50 percent if I'd had someone guiding me. Thank goodness Don eventually entered my life, but that wasn't until ten years in. Everybody needs something a little different from a business coach. If you skew toward the business owner end of the spectrum, you likely need a coach to help grow your confidence and light a fire in you. If you're more of a serial entrepreneur like me, you need someone to reign you back in and help you make wise choices. My wife isn't a business coach, but in those early days, I was fortunate to have her in my ear helping me see that now might not be the right time for everything and to plan things out first.

The most rewarding thing I do now is to be that mentor for others and to help them avoid making so many of the mistakes that I did. Just yesterday I talked to a group of landscapers, and all of them want to become entrepreneurs. They want to stop working in the day-to-day things in their business and start working on it. They also want a better quality of life, which we'll talk about shortly. But their main hang-up is that nobody has given them the tools to make this shift. They aren't hiring C-suite people or managers, and they aren't delegating. They're out in the field doing all of the work. They have no idea how to begin, and most importantly, they haven't yet developed the mindset necessary to take the leap.

QUALITY OF LIFE

One of the biggest wins of entrepreneurship is the improvement in your quality of life (usually). The landscapers I just mentioned want to grow and scale to make more money, of course. Most of us want that. But what they really want is to stop digging ditches. They want to stop being the only one available at 10:00 a.m. on a Sunday when a client has an emergent need. They want their income to not be so tied to their working hours so that they can live more life and enjoy their families. Most business owners work *so much*. They don't have any work-life balance. The life of a business owner may be more predictable in that they aren't taking many risks, trying new things, or relying on others as much, but it's also quite exhausting when the entire business rests on you. An entrepreneur is not okay with that. They don't want things to stay the same. They want to keep going and maximize their potential.

It's clear by now that I always wanted to be an entrepreneur. I had great goals from the start. But a huge factor in me finally taking off the apron, besides finally listening to Don, was my lack of work-life balance. I made sacrifices I would not wish on any of my employees. Family is everything to me. It was my first pillar and the Y behind everything I do. I was in the battle of my new business and it needed me. It couldn't survive without me. I had to finally loosen the reins and begin delegating not only for the sake of my business but also for the sake of my family and for my well-being. This doesn't mean that entrepreneurship is easy. It's hard and stressful. It requires faith and risk-taking. It can also be quite lonely. But when you begin to think like an entrepreneur and step out of your business so that you can work on it, you create some freedom. You remove yourself as the bottleneck for all systems and processes. You empower others to make decisions and to execute on the experience creation, which in turn results in a better life for yourself. When you're a business owner, it's hard to see the forest for the trees. You're actually dead smack in the middle of the trees. The path to being an entrepreneur starts by working your way out of the forest.

Going from business owner to entrepreneur, and potentially to serial entrepreneur way down the road if that's your ultimate goal, requires a certain set of skills and knowledge. This is one of the most important things I teach my clients. In order to be an entrepreneur, there are skills you need to either innately have or learn: the ability to take risks and to fail well.

RISK

When I speak at entrepreneurial classes at universities, the first question I ask is, "How many of you are risk-takers?" Usually 80 percent of the class will raise their hands. Being a business owner is risky, but it's the level of risk you take that determines your growth. You should know your fundamentals, like setting up your systems and understanding your three pillars to help mitigate risk. You should also know your numbers and have a plan. All wise business owners take calculated risks, not stupid risks.

All wise business owners take calculated risks, not stupid risks.

But when it comes to scaling and growth, almost everything you do has some element of risk. There is no sure thing. We just do our best with the information we have and jump. An aversion to risk might be the number one thing that holds business owners back. Taking risks builds our confidence. It shows us that we can try something new and survive or not. It is a defining moment in business.

FAILURE

I then ask the same students to raise their hands if they like to fail, and fewer than 10 percent do. I then tell them, "If you don't like to fail, then this might not be the class for you." These brand-new risks you are taking as you build your confidence will absolutely lead to some failure. That's just a fact. Learning to fail well is essential to becoming an entrepreneur because you are going to fail. But don't be too scared by this. For me, there are two types of failures: micro and macro. What we're talking about here is aiming for micro failures. A micro failure is something that won't cripple your business. It could look like trying a new product in your business, depending on how much your products cost, of course. For me, adding a new item to our menu that does not do well is a micro failure. It won't sink my business. It's not a huge risk to add a different kind of pizza. It's a loss I can withstand. There are degrees to this, but the simplest way to put it is that a micro failure is a calculated risk that you can withstand financially. If it fails, how much will it cost you? Do you have the people and processes to execute it? Will you and your business be okay if it tanks?

On the contrary, a macro failure will sink you. I almost experienced a macro failure when I opened a bakery when I was young. Sal was a great baker, and I cared for him. I made an emotional decision and thought to myself, *I'm going to put this guy in business.* But I wasn't prepared. I didn't have a coach guiding me, and it didn't work. I almost lost everything. Putting $600,000 into opening a business when you don't know your three pillars, don't have your systems in place, and don't have a defined brand is a recipe for a macro failure. Depending on your situation, losing that much money could mean losing everything. If you have a family to support, this is something to think even harder about, because others are depending on you. A good business coach helps you avoid macro failures and will often push you toward micro failures. Too often we associate failure with negative outcomes. But failure teaches us so much! And most important for entrepreneurs, failure builds confidence. Often, to make the jump from business owner to entrepreneur, you need to get your feet wet with failure. You need to experience some small bumps and learn that you'll survive so that you can get back up and try again. I realized so much from that bakery failure. It was one of the hardest and best lessons I learned in my career. The very next day, I got back up and kept moving forward. I decided it would make me better, and it did. The wisdom I learned from the bakery has helped me with every business deal since then.

How well do you fail? How do you handle failure? Think back to when you were a kid playing sports. If you lost, did you get back out there and try again? Learning to fail well is a skill you can learn, but it's also good to examine your background and personality to see how easy or hard this is for you. I wrestled in high school, and whenever I got pinned down, I practiced even harder the next day to make sure that didn't happen the next week. All of my daughters swim. Whenever my oldest would lose a race, the next day at practice, she examined her stroke and strategy to see what she could improve. Failure is an opportunity. Learning to fail well may take more effort for some than for others. But it won't kill you; instead, it'll make you better and stronger. I honestly believe I have learned more from my failures than from my successes.

ENTREPRENEURIAL RESILIENCE

These two skills, tolerating risk and failing well, are both important for creating entrepreneurial resilience. Resilience is the capacity to recover quickly from difficulties. It's toughness. In entrepreneurship, resilience is essential. Your capacity to get back up when you fall is what will keep you going. If it takes you a long time to recover when you fail, you're out of business. Every time you take a risk or experience a micro failure and then get back up to live another day is one more notch in

> **In entrepreneurship, resilience is essential.**

your resilience belt. All of these things work together toward your confidence and success. And because you know I just can't help it, let's bring it back around to the three pillars again. It's critically important to have a clear vision and a deep understanding of your brand. Those fundamentals that we worked on in chapter 1 (that I told you not to move on from without mastering—have you done that?) are what give you direction and calculation when you take those risks. They also work to give you confidence as you leap into the unknown but exciting world of entrepreneurship.

Do you think you're ready? Are you ready to start risking some micro failures to make steps toward scaling your business? Really look deep inside and be honest with yourself. Can you weather the storm if it comes? Entrepreneurial resilience is where the rubber really meets the road. If we were sitting together in person, you'd be able to see my body language as I get fired up talking about this and encouraging entrepreneurs. You can do it! You just have to start taking some calculated risks and take the first step forward. What's your next step? What's one small risk you can take today? I want you to think about it and write it down. Rip a page out of this book for all I care. Put it up where you can see it and make sure you follow through. Confidence follows action, which is why those micro failures are so important. These skills can be learned. All you have to do is start.

ACTION STEPS

1. Be honest with yourself: Are you a business owner or an entrepreneur? (Or even a serial entrepreneur?) What do you want to be?

2. Are you content with your quality of life? Do you think you have work-life balance? In your dream workday, what would you change?

3. Do you consider yourself risk-averse? When was the last time you took a risk? How did you handle it?

4. How do you handle failure? Name one micro failure in your business that you're willing to accept today. Make a plan to take a risk and execute it.

5. Do you need to hire a business coach? Do you have the support you need to achieve your goals?

6. Identify one thing that would help you build entrepreneurial resilience.

7. Are your systems defined well enough so that your employees avoid macro failures?

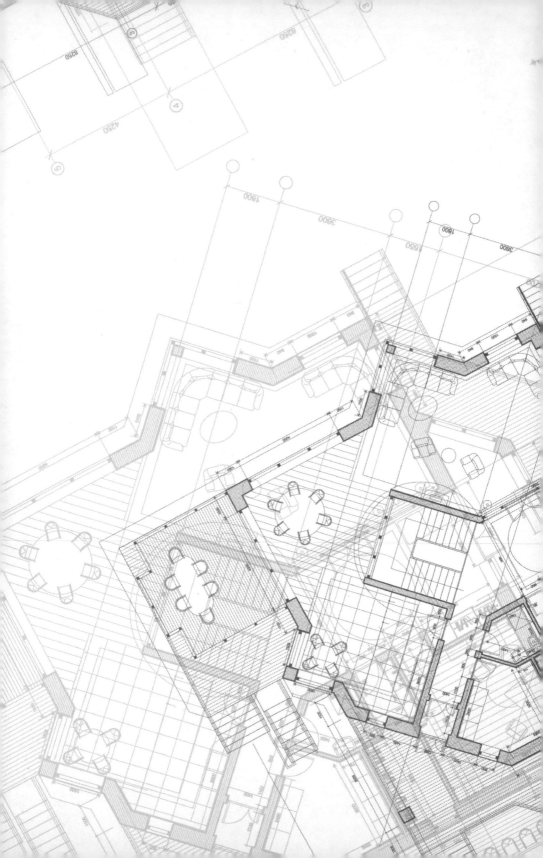

Delegation Built to Scale

WITHOUT TRUST, FAILURE WILL NEVER HAPPEN.

When I started my construction company back in the day, my truck was loaded up with the tools I needed for every job I went to. I was just a solopreneur in that respect. My restaurants were running well without me (systems!), so I took on a new challenge. I was doing everything from laying tile to hanging drywall, framing walls, and even sweeping floors. I was doing a damn good job, too. But as my business grew, I couldn't do it alone anymore. I had learned this lesson before in my other businesses, but once again I had to let go and delegate. I took all the tools out of my truck and started hiring subcontractors while I managed them. It's no surprise that this is when that business took off.

What if I said that you could accomplish 1000 percent of the tasks you needed to do every day? I say this a lot on stage, and every time someone comments, "Well, I could certainly do one hundred percent, but I can't do one thousand percent. There's no such thing." That's only true if you try to do all ten of the tasks yourself. But if you delegate 90 percent of everything you have to do to someone else, suddenly you can accomplish a lot more. Now you have to do only 10 percent of those original tasks, and you can take on other big picture things. And then perhaps that person also delegates 90 percent of their tasks to someone else, which then allows them to accomplish more. This may sound simplistic, but it is amazing how often I teach this. This is how you multiply yourself. This is the power of delegation.

You can't do this alone. You just can't. Maybe you could be a business owner by yourself. But even that would be hard. And you certainly can't be an entrepreneur alone. You need help, and you need to loosen the reins on what you do. If you walked out of your business right now and left for a whole day, could it function without you? Have you passed off all the tasks that can be done by someone else so that you aren't the bottleneck in your business anymore? If I had to guess, I'd say that delegation is where most entrepreneurs fail. Either because they do it poorly or because they don't do it at all. I've created dozens of businesses myself and have coached plenty of others, so take it from me: This is the fundamental issue most business owners struggle with. It goes back to the heart of this book that we've touched on in every chapter: You have to stop working in your business and start working on it. Put your talents to their best use and be the visionary. You have to do like I did and take your apron off. Stop making the pizzas, and let somebody else do it.

THE COUNTERINTUITIVE NATURE OF DELEGATION

There are two main reasons people don't delegate: pride and fear. Pride because they believe they can do it better themselves and fear because they are unsure of what will happen when they hand off responsibility. Delegation is hard; I won't sugarcoat that. It's also a learned skill. I'll explain how to do it in this chapter, but the only thing that will truly teach you how to delegate is to experience doing it. Like everything in business, you'll learn the most from taking action and also from making mistakes. You won't always hire the right person for the right task. Sometimes the person you hire might not be great at the position. But one of the best things about business is when you hire, delegate, and train someone and then realize that they're better than you ever were at that position. It's so rewarding! I'm no longer the pizza maker in our business. I shouldn't be. That's not my job,

> **Like everything in business, you'll learn the most from taking action and also from making mistakes.**

and others have taken that task and improved on it. At some point you have to let your pride go and begin to hand off your tasks for the sake of the growth of your business. You won't reach your goals otherwise. Plus, you'll get to invest in and develop others, which is truly one of the most fun parts of business.

People are afraid of a few different things when it comes to delegation. They're afraid everything will fall apart without them. If you've built out your systems, that shouldn't happen. Yes, delegation takes some practice, but with the right systems, you and your employees are set up for success. That's why we covered systems first. Sometimes people are afraid of spending the money to hire and pay others. Delegation is counterintuitive like this: You have to let go to gain more, and you have to pay more to make more. It was June 1993 when I opened my first Ynot Italian restaurant, but I can tell you that in the almost thirty years since then, I have hired thousands of people, fired a few too, and lost and made millions. And one of the things I'm proudest of is that I have been able to surround myself with so many great employees. You have to begin trusting someone else so that you can work on the big picture tasks that only you can do. It's scary at first and can even seem wise to keep doing things yourself to "save money." But that's not how entrepreneurship works. Freeing up your time is incredibly valuable. Trust yourself that if you pay someone $14 an hour to start cleaning your floors, or $80,000 to run your sales force, that will free you up to find ways to make an extra $1,000 a day. Or if you're like me, open another business. Have faith and be positive. You can do this.

Melissa is a massage therapist and one of my coaching clients. She'd been in business for seven years when she sought me out because she wanted to expand. Melissa and I are very different. Some of my clients come to me because we have similar energy and they align with that. And some come especially because of our differences. This is Melissa. She is much more of a thinker than a doer and had been scared about expansion for years. She was comfortable as a solo entrepreneur. During our first call, I asked her why she wanted to expand. "Because I want to make more money," she said. That was partially true, but I knew that wasn't fully it. Melissa lit up when she spoke about her business and clients. I knew there was more to it. I had to ask her three times before she finally told me that she's incredibly passionate about helping people feel better. After so many years in business, her hands ached. She had problems with her thumbs. She wanted to help more people, but she was simply tapped out. She couldn't handle any more on her own, and to keep her dreams alive, she needed to expand.

I knew it was time for delegation, but first we had to dig into the three pillars. It always comes back to that, my friends. After weeks of working through the exercise, Melissa decided that her three pillars are tranquility, mobility, and focus. I started asking questions about her clients and what they felt after a session. She said they felt like they were in a state of nirvana. Her business was currently named Mama's Medicine because of the healing association with motherly touch. But after diving into her mind, it didn't quite align with her pillars, so she changed it to Nirvana Massage. I have a reputation for changing the names of businesses. I think people try to get too clever with it or name their business before they really have their brand worked out. Anyway, with her pillars as our guide and her new name decided, it was time to start delegating. She was able to use the three pillars to articulate her vision so that she could scale. Melissa decided to not fully hire employees but to train other massage therapists to work under her as independent contractors. There are lots of financial and tax reasons for this, but the big picture is that this helped Melissa achieve her growth and financial goals the fastest while keeping things tranquil and focused. She developed a system for teaching her method to others and maintaining the unique value that she brings to the business. When I coach delegation, I take people through the four steps of doing it successfully. This is exactly what I did with Melissa. I am so proud of her. She took the leap from business owner to entrepreneur. Let's get into it.

THE FOUR STEPS OF DELEGATION

STEP 1: IDENTIFY THE RIGHT TASK

The reason we covered systems before delegation is because you cannot delegate without knowing what tasks you need to outsource, right? You can't hire someone new or hand off tasks to an existing employee if you have no idea what to have them do. Take a look at the systems you created in chapter 2. Examine that list of things you do all day. What can be done by someone else? Can you stop cleaning your store? Can you stop doing your own accounting? What about making products? I'm sure there are plenty of things that you're doing right now that can be transferred to someone else. I tell my clients to make a list of twenty things they can delegate and then start with the first ten. The whole purpose of codifying what you do every day and what needs to happen in your business is so that you can eventually hand off most of those tasks to someone else. We're trying to multiply you so that you can use your brain for bigger things. Identify the tasks to delegate.

Start with the small, easy ones. When your child is learning to walk, you don't let them first try it on the concrete where they could bust their face. You put them on carpet where they're more comfortable and less likely to get hurt. Remember micro failure versus macro failure. Not every task is created equal. Defining the complexity of each one is imperative. This will be important in the next step.

STEP 2: IDENTIFY THE RIGHT PERSON

This one might be a little trickier, as humans are more complicated than tasks. As you scroll through that list of tasks to delegate, begin taking notes on what qualities a person must have to be the best candidate. Our hostesses and waiters need to be friendly. They need to like people and enjoy talking. They need to smile and be warm. They also need to be able to stay on their feet for hours at a time and move quickly. They need to be solution-driven problem solvers who can think quickly. It's not enough to have identified the right task; the task and the person need to match. Sometimes you can identify the right task but delegate it to the entirely wrong person. If Sally is afraid of heights, don't send her up a ladder to paint the ceiling. Sometimes it's as simple as that.

What qualities does a person require for the first task on your list? We'll get into this a bit more in the training chapter. What level of experience or training do they need? What kind of personality should they have? What outcome are you looking for in this position? The employee's mindset matters a lot. Make sure that your desired outcome also matches their desire as well as their ability to do it.

One of my owner-operators named Chico might be my best hire ever. Back in 2009, Chico was in college. He had married young and needed a job to support his growing family. His dad had worked for me for a couple of years and suggested that Chico do the same. He wasn't super into the idea at the time but decided to take the job for a few years until he could join the military. Fifteen years later, he's still crushing it. I saw something in Chico. He worked incredibly hard and always wanted to take on more responsibility. He completed all the tasks that others left unfinished. I knew there was great potential in him. The funny thing is, he didn't even speak to me for the first two years. He just kept his mouth shut and his head down and did the work. I kept approaching him and trying to get to know him. Slowly he opened up. He grew up in an environment where you don't talk to the boss; you just do your work and go home. But that's not at all how I operate. I am a communicator. Every day I asked him about his goals and talked to him about managing other people.

Soon I promoted him to kitchen manager, then general manager, and now he's an owner-operator of a Ynot Italian location making millions, but he struggled with delegation for a long time. He was great at being delegated to, but as he rose through the ranks of my business, it became more and more important for him to delegate, and he just wouldn't let go. His instinct to finish others' tasks or to take over when things were going wrong stunted his ability to delegate. He was a micromanager and a perfectionist. He always wanted to do every job, and he was good at it too, which is why I kept delegating more to him. But eventually he was high up enough that he needed to learn the art of delegation for himself. He worked for me for twelve years before he finally said he was going to start hiring more people so that the restaurant could grow. It took Chico a long time to let people fail so that he could grow. Like Don did with me, I told Chico to take the apron off every time I saw him. Delegation is the hardest thing to learn for a business owner.

There was a lot of investing and training that went into Chico developing those skills, but it all started because I delegated to him. I needed help and could see that he was capable. He was the right person for those tasks, and the more he did well, the more tasks I passed onto him. He is teachable, honorable, and hardworking. Taking a long-term employee and giving them the opportunity to become an owner has been one of the most rewarding things I have done in business. Seeing him thrive and become a trusted friend has been a great honor. Finding the right person cannot be taken lightly. Invest in choosing the right person for the job, and you will be one step closer.

STEP 3: SET EXPECTATIONS

This is another area where systemizing your systems should come in handy. Remember when we identified all those Ys in chapter 2? That's how you set expectations for your employees once you decide on the task and the person. You have to let them know exactly what they need to do, train them, and explain why they need to do it. If your systems are well defined, your success rate will be much greater. Most managers fail at this step. This is an area where they need to take their time. Does the manager completely understand the task, and do they know how to articulate the process? I hear business owners complaining about millennials a lot, but this group of employees has been my favorite. All they want to know is why. When I was growing up, asking why was frowned upon. This is when investing in your employees will pay off. Show them the Y.

Not too long ago, I asked one of my managers to run my staff meeting of seventy people and he said, "No problem, I've got it." I told him I would not be speaking at this meeting. I wanted to give him a chance to run it. The next morning we sat in front of the entire staff, and for thirty minutes all he did was degrade them by going over problems and policies that the employees were not doing right. I was highly frustrated because that is not how I run my meetings. At this point, I could not embarrass him in front of seventy people, so I let him finish the meeting. I started to criticize myself first. Did I set the right expectation for this meeting? Did I train him on how to run a meeting properly? I realized that this is where I failed.

I sat him down when the meeting finished, and for the next two hours, we went over how to run a meeting properly. I showed him how to ask questions. For example, instead of driving the policy down their throats, I asked him, "When you walk in in the morning and the place is a mess, how does that make you feel?" Giving examples at meetings helps employees relate and have an open mind. It was my fault he degraded them that day. I thoroughly apologized to him for not setting him up for success. I didn't invest in my employee. A month later, he ran another meeting and crushed it. He was so excited. The employees thanked him for a great meeting. Setting an expectation properly gives your employees confidence because when they finish the job after doing it correctly, they will be ready for the next task you give them. Every time you delegate a task and the employee doesn't do it to your standard, you need to criticize yourself first. You need to make sure you set the proper expectations before you release them.

This step (and this whole process) is also guided by the pillar of integrity in my construction company. Because the three pillars have everything to do with the experience you're trying to create. Last week I was on a construction job, and I asked my employee John to sweep the floor and make sure there were no nails laying around or lumber on the floors. I needed it perfect before tomorrow. He asked me why and I told him, "The owners are coming here every day to inspect the job, and the last thing I want is for them to get hurt when they walk through the house. Not to mention I want them to be proud of what they see when they come in." Now there's a good why. I set the expectation. I set the why. I clearly explained the result I was looking for from John *and* the experience I was trying to create for the client. I didn't just tell him to sweep the floor. That's what dictators do. Understand that you need to explain the why.

STEP 4: FOLLOW UP

This is where delegation either lives or dies. This is often the step where success happens or the delegation falls apart completely. Not many people follow up. They identify the task, pass it off to someone, give them a few directions, and let them be. After you've handed over the task and given the person a fair amount of time to execute on it, you need to come back around, evaluate how they did, and help them improve. Return to the previous steps. What was the task that you outlined? Who did you assign it to? Did you set the expectation? Did all of that go well? Did you get the result you were expecting? There are two parts to the follow through. The first is what I outlined earlier—the black-and-white part of the process. Did this work or not? But remember that we're dealing with humans because we're all in the same business—the people business. There's a good chance that person thinks they've done a great job, and there's a good chance you see room for improvement. That's perfectly fine. People need to be helped along and shown where they went wrong. But …

BONUS STEP 5: RADICAL RESPONSIBILITY

Here's a bonus step for you that might just be the most important one. If the employee didn't execute the task correctly and you didn't get the results you were looking for, examine yourself first. Most people's instinct is to criticize others. *They didn't do this right. They didn't understand. They didn't have the right skills.* All of that may be true. But you hired them, you created the task, and you created the system. The buck stops with you. Maybe you need to update your standard operating procedures. Maybe you picked the wrong person. That's not the person's fault; it's yours. Perhaps you have a great system but nobody understands it but you. Guess what? That's nobody's fault but your own. As entrepreneurs, our mindset should be radical responsibility. You've been given a job and a duty to motivate people. It's an honor to encourage people, help them grow, and create a great experience for them and for your customers. That's the ultimate goal we're trying to accomplish, right? Think about the guy at the construction job who I asked to clean the floors. When the owners walked through the next day, they remarked on how clean the house was. So I made a point to tell him that and compliment his work. Now he feels great about his effort, and he knows how he contributed to the overall success of the project. He's empowered and confident. He's also more likely to ask for more to do and be more willing to try new tasks.

The second people are disempowered and unsatisfied with their job, look to yourself before you blame them. This is hard to do, but it is a must. Managers are more apt to call someone stupid or fire an employee than to criticize themselves. As entrepreneurs, CEOs, and leaders, we carry a lot of stress. We do all kinds of things nobody else even knows about. I know it can be tempting to think, *They aren't cleaning the floors right, but that isn't my problem.* But it is, and this is where training your manager to set expectations thoroughly will pay dividends. Your employees' problems are yours, but you can make them your opportunities instead! Remember that solutions create results.

LET PEOPLE FAIL

Let's talk about micro and macro failures again because this is another place they come into play. Nobody is going to be perfect at the job you give them. You can pick the best person for it, and they're still going to mess up, especially in the beginning. When I'm delegating, I choose the task, find the right person, set the expectation, and then get my mindset right that they won't do it perfectly. And they won't do it exactly like me. A micro failure is a failure that won't severely hurt your business but that lets you empower your employee. So many entrepreneurs struggle with expecting and allowing micro failures from others. I'd never tell an employee that I expect them to fail, of course. That would be terrible. But the truth is, to some extent I do expect it. Hell, I fail at things when I'm new at them. So I don't give them tasks that could lead to macro failures. If someone at one of my restaurants makes a pizza wrong, that's a micro failure. It's no big deal. We just make a new pizza. If one of my framers on a construction site frames a bearing wall wrong, the whole project is in big trouble. That's a macro failure that is hard to recover from.

Letting people learn from micro failures isn't just for them; it's for you, too. If you don't allow for micro failures, one of these days you'll end up with a macro failure and you'll quit delegating all together. *See, I was right! Nobody else can do this like I can; they just mess it up. I'll do it myself.* That's the mentality that happens when you delegate a task that for one reason or another leads to a macro failure. You lose your confidence in delegation and your business stops growing. It's very common, and I see it a lot. Managers end up staying at work till 3:00 a.m. because someone messed up royally and now they're too scared to delegate again.

Allowing people to fail is part of learning and investing in them. Empathy is an underrated skill in business and must be trained. It's different from when I grew up. The employees want to know Y and that you care. I'm sure you fail regularly in your job. I know I do. You must give your employees the same chance. When people fail, help them learn from it. Follow up and educate them about what went wrong and how to fix it. Then implement that into your systems. Environments in which people are allowed to fail foster growth and trust. If you're employing people and not giving them space to fail, you're simply hiring them, not investing in them. When you follow up and motivate someone by showing them how they contribute to the whole, you gain their buy-in. That's when the magic can really happen in a business. Employees become so invested in the success of the business that they have a sense of ownership and begin figuring out how to improve things all on their own.

WE'RE ALL 98.6 DEGREES

I want to bring it back to mindset again for a minute. It might sound overly simple, but when it comes to delegation, it's important to continue to remember that you're dealing with people. *I know, I know, Tony. Of course we're all humans!* But you'd be amazed how many bosses think they're delegating to machines that they can just plug into any job and get a good result. Humans are complicated. They have per-

The whole point of delegation is to be able to scale.

sonalities, attitudes, families, problems, etc. Do you know what's going on in your employees' lives? There's a fine line to walk here, and you don't want to get overly personal, but these things really matter. Do they have a sick kid? Are they going through a divorce? There's the four-step system I outlined in this chapter and then there's this human element, too. When employees fail, ask the question, Is everything okay? So many times when I was young, I didn't know how to pause and think about this. I thought people were machines. They're not computers that you can program and expect to operate the same every time. You have to allow them to fail, and you have to allow them to be human.

The whole point of delegation is to be able to scale; that's where this is ultimately going. You're moving from business owner to entrepreneur, and the way you do that is by mastering delegation and empowering your employees. You cannot scale without people. I said it at the start of this chapter, and I'll say it again: You can't do this alone. Don't be the eighty-five-year-old in my neighborhood who owns the restaurant and still works at the cash register because he doesn't trust anyone else to handle the money. You won't grow without delegation. You won't accomplish your goals. And you'll miss out on the fun of taking other people along on this wild and crazy ride with you. You need to master the art of delegation!

⚐ ACTION STEPS

1. Look at the list of systems you created in chapter 2. Pick ten things on it that you can delegate to someone else.

2. Do you already know employees who can take on those tasks, or do you need to hire someone else? I encourage you to first try to hand off a few tasks to an existing employee. But if you need to hire someone, turn the page, because we're talking about that in chapter 5.

3. Ask one person who works for you today if they understand the why behind what they do. Do they know the reasons behind each task? Take a minute to find out and explain it to them if you need to.

4. Teach your managers to look at themselves before criticizing the employee.

5. Ask someone about their life. Find out how they really are. Be a human being and treat them the way you'd like to be treated. Bonus points if this is an entry-level employee.

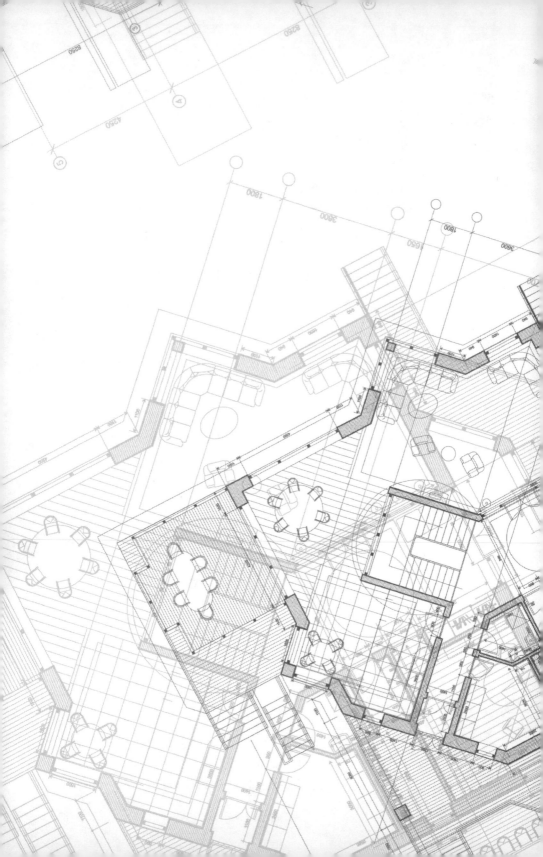

CHAPTER 5

Training: Invest in Your People

INVEST IN YOUR EMPLOYEES, AND THEY WILL INVEST IN YOU!

In March 2015, a Germanwings plane crashed into a remote mountain range in the Alps, killing 150 people. The first thing everyone wanted to know after that tragedy was, How could this happen? Was it mechanical failure? Politically motivated or perhaps terrorism? It turns out that, sadly, none of that was to blame. The reason for the crash was entirely human. The investigation got a little messy, but there are a few things we now know are true about the pilot and the airline's training policies. Part of the hiring and training process is to make sure that every pilot has a Class 1 medical certificate to ensure that they are physically and mentally fit to fly. The Germanwings pilot was struggling heavily with depression, and the investigation showed that the airline knew and did nothing to intervene. Obviously airlines are a high-risk industry where employees have the potential to put others' lives in jeopardy. But regardless of your industry, training, both technical and emotional, has huge implications. You must be sure people are equipped in every possible way to execute on the tasks assigned to them.

The pilot should have been monitored and helped. He should have had more regular follow-ups and evaluations. It's easy to say that it's solely the pilot's fault that he crashed. But I say it's a failure of the entire training system and, more specifically, a failure of that company to invest in its people. That's what this chapter is about. But before we get started, it's time for a midbook gut check. So far we've covered the three pillars and how those are a deep dive into your brand and why they are essential to everything else that comes next. We talked about the mindset shift needed to go from a business owner to an entrepreneur. And we've covered systemizing your systems and the importance of delegation. But let me ask you this: Do you know why we did it that way? Do you know why we did it in that order? Why have I insisted that you not move on before you first comprehend the chapter you just read? Because this is all leading somewhere. It's all to set you up for scaling. We're building a house here, and like every structure, you have to do it in the right order or it'll all come crashing down. Training and marketing are the two most expensive things you'll ever do in your business. So you better make sure your house is in order before you move on.

If you don't have your systems in place, how are you ever going to know what to delegate? If you don't know what to delegate, how are you ever going to know who to hire and how to train them? And if your brand isn't established and your employees are not properly trained to create an amazing experience for your customer, guess what's going to happen? Either you're going to waste a ton of money on marketing and no one will come, or maybe people will come, but because you didn't build the proper foundation, those customers won't have a great experience and will never come back, which is probably even worse than no one coming in the first place. All of that marketing is useless. Do you see where I'm going with this? Training always comes before marketing. So let's get into it.

Everybody wants a new customer to come through the door, right? That's marketing, which we'll get into in the next chapter. That's why we do this, so we can share what we're passionate about with the world. We want people to come! We want to sell more cars or jewelry or houses. So you create a fancy marketing plan … and perhaps the only people who see it are you, your advertising agency, and your customers. It never makes its way to your employees, especially the entry-level employees interacting with customers. The way you execute on that promise you made in your marketing is through training your people. That's how you execute on a granular basis. Your marketing program will succeed so much faster and more efficiently because of your training.

Imagine if Apple came out with a new iPhone, and as a sales associate, you had no idea what the new features were. Nobody told you, and nobody trained you. Customers are coming into the store in droves asking about the new product and all of its capabilities. They clearly saw that fancy marketing plan the higher-ups made. But you haven't. You have no idea what they're talking about and can't help them. And you certainly can't sell them something you know nothing about. You likely work on commission, so not being able to sell iPhones is really disappointing for you. You get frustrated. Your employer *really* gets frustrated. And you want to leave. That's expensive for your employer to hire and train someone else, and it's a huge bummer for you because now you're out of a job and you have to start all over again somewhere else. This is obviously an outlandish example. Apple trains its employees amazingly well, and everyone I've interacted with has been very knowledgeable. But I use it specifically because I want to drive this point home: If there is a huge disconnect between your marketing and your training, your employees won't succeed, which means you won't succeed. Your company should be focused on creating an experience, and the only way you do this is by investing in your employees through training them.

THE EMPLOYEE AVATAR

In chapter 1 we talked about the customer avatar. Remember, that's your ideal customer. This is a common business term that most people have heard. What are their needs, wants, desires? What are they looking for when they come to your business? What do they feel? Similarly, when hiring, delegating, and especially training, it's important to create your employee avatar. After you decide who your ideal customer is, you need to decide who is the best kind of person to sell it and how to train them to get the customer experience and desired outcome that you're looking for. Remember Sophie, my coaching client with the medical recruiting business? Her customers are urgent care centers and doctors' offices. The doctors she places in these facilities don't officially work for Sophie, but they act as her employees in that they are placed and vetted by her. And if all goes well, they become employees of the centers and offices. During a coaching call, I asked her, "What does your customer want? Speed? Friendliness? Empathy?" That's the customer avatar. But now you need to take the doctors you have and create an employee avatar to match. She ended up developing three categories of doctors: ones who are solely focused on speed, entirely compassionate doctors focused on empathy, and some well-rounded docs who consider themselves decent at both. There is value in all of these. For the sake of the patient, some places need to prioritize speed. Emergency rooms may fall into this category. Some specialty doctors' offices are concerned only with whether their patients feel heard and cared for. They may not even want it to be a fast experience. And some places fall in between.

Understanding these customer avatars helped Sophie create employee avatars. Though customer avatars are a much-talked-about part of business, employee avatars are often overlooked. Once you understand what your customers' expectations are, you can train your people to meet them. If your customer wants a fancy sports car with leather seats and all top-of-the-line features, they have different expectations than if they were buying a low-end car, right? Your employees will be interacting with high-income earners who are spending a lot of money. They want something specific. Who is the ideal employee avatar to match that customer avatar? They probably dress very sharply and speak well. They can hold a conversation and know the importance of playing the long game in sales rather than a quick pitch. They're not focused on speed but on the quality of the interaction with the customer.

When you walk into a Starbucks, you'll notice an eclectic mix of baristas. Many of them have tattoos and gauges and are dressed very casually. Some of them even have funky hair and facial piercings. This is great! That's Starbucks' brand. They are a hipster, casual kind of joint. It's cool; it's the vibe. They value inclusivity and are located all over the world, so they want to represent many people. But that same employee avatar would not work at my locally owned and operated family Italian restaurant in Virginia. The customer who walked into Starbucks at 8:00 a.m. for a coffee could walk into my restaurant for dinner and see the exact same employee and be surprised, when at Starbucks they didn't think twice. Why? It's all about expectations. My employee avatar is different from Starbucks' because my brand and customer avatar are completely different. Even the same group of painters can be perceived differently from house to house. If I bring a group of disheveled, mismatched painters who aren't in uniform to a $3 million house, they will be judged differently. That customer avatar expects a clean-cut group with a custom logo shirt tucked in. But for a company building track homes where the customer just wants the house up as quickly as possible and at a lower price, they probably don't care as much. Your customer avatar dictates your employee avatar. And the way you get those to align is through training.

The three pillars define who your customer and brand are, and training is about getting your employees aligned with the customer avatar to create an experience through your employees. When we get into marketing in the next chapter, you'll understand how we combine these ideas—marketing to your customer avatar and ensuring that you have the right employee avatar to execute on the marketing promises you made to those customers.

INVEST IN PEOPLE

The biggest thing people misunderstand about training is that real training is investing in your people.

The biggest thing people misunderstand about training is that real training is investing in your people. I don't hire people, I invest in them, and I expect employees to invest in me. If you're not investing in your people, you're not doing it right. When I tell employees I'm investing in them, sometimes they look at me like I'm crazy. But this is where culture training starts. They're keeping my business going and helping put food on my table just the same as I put food on theirs. Every single one of us, even the solopreneurs, are in the people business. You've already heard me say that throughout this book, right? But I don't just mean that about customers. I mean it when it comes to investing in our employees. You are in the people business in every way. The business *of* people. If you're not taking the time to invest in your employees, then I don't know why you're in business. Good leaders invest in their people.

Have you seen the movie *You've Got Mail*? I have three daughters, so I certainly have. I've spent more time than I'd like to admit watching rom-coms. There's a scene toward the end where Joe Fox comes over to apologize to Kathleen Kelly. His big Barnes and Noble-like bookstore, Fox Books, has just put her small local bookstore, the Shop around the Corner, out of business. Her mom started it and handed it down to her. Joe sits down beside Kathleen and says, "It wasn't personal; it's business." And she replies, "What does that mean, anyway? Whatever else anything is, it ought to begin by being personal." That's how I view business. I know we have to make smart decisions, pay attention to numbers, and think logically. But business is personal because we're all just people, customers and employees alike. You're hiring someone with a personality and goals and a life. Invest in them.

THE EMPLOYEE EXPERIENCE

Every day at 5:00 p.m., my seven waitstaff members have a meeting. We all stand in a circle, and I ask them how many servers are on the floor tonight. They will all say none. I say, "What?" And they reply, "We are experience creators!" Bang! We've talked a lot about creating an experience for our customers. Your employees aren't just employees. They're also experience creators. And just like how we took the customer avatar and flipped it to create an employee avatar, I want to do the same thing for the experience. We're creating not only an external experience for our customers but also an internal experience for our employees. Your staff is having an experience when they come to work and interact with each other. They want to work with people they like and to learn and grow from them. That's what I want for them, too. If my employees aren't seeking growth, then they're doing it wrong.

It's important that your employees understand that they're creating an experience for each other, too. When I was coaching an architecture firm, I asked the owner, "What do you call the people who draw your homes?" He replied that they were designers. I said, "Imagine if you called them experience creators instead." He wanted to know why. "When they design the kitchen, do they think of how the sun will come through the windows? If the sun hits the kitchen table in the morning while I'm drinking my coffee, I'll be mad that it's in my eyes. Does the pool have full sun all day? Don't you think the homeowner will want that as they lay out back?" He saw my point. These details matter. They dictate the entire experience a homeowner will have while living there. An architect can design a house, but it takes an experience creator to design a home.

Affirmations like experience creator only work if you use them daily. You need to dive deep! You cannot expect this from your employees unless you've trained them in it every day. Talk about the three pillars, and remind them of their role and the outcomes we're looking for. Training, like systemizing, never stops. What we're talking about when we say the employee experience is the personality of the brand. Your three pillars are your mission and vision. But the internal piece of that is the company culture created by your three pillars. Your training creates this culture.

TRAINING BACKWARD

The three pillars for my Italian restaurant business are family, quality, and community. We are an experience brand. So are you, by the way. We don't sell food; we deliver experiences. I say this all the time to my C-suite, and even they often bring it right back down to ground level. We'll get to the granular piece of the brand process later. But if you're thinking that way right now, stop. As we move along, remember this mindset. I want the cooks in my company to understand that every time they make a meal, they're creating an experience for the guests. When they bag up take-out food, what is the experience that customer thinks about when they open it up? How did we make a difference to their family? That's what we're going for here.

Not long ago my daughter bought her first house, and we went to a very expensive restaurant to celebrate. It took us forty-five minutes to get our drinks and another forty-five for our server to take our order. The food was super salty, and the whole experience was bad. The entire time we were out, we weren't talking about this huge milestone for my daughter. Instead, we were saying things like "I can't believe we don't have our drinks" and "My food isn't great." They weren't selling us food that night; they were selling us an experience. And it was a bad one. The focus should have been on this huge celebration but instead it was on the terrible experience. That's a failure in training.

But how do we train this? How do we train our employees not only to execute on important daily tasks like sweeping the floors but also to understand that they're contributing to an important experience the customer is having with us? How do we train them to create a great experience? That night at the restaurant, they might have delivered on the customer avatar piece. They knew who their customer was and effectively got us in the door. But they failed on the employee avatar part. Where exactly did it fail? Was it the cooks? Was it the server? Was it the management? We'll never know because I'm never going back there. But the point is, you need to be asking yourself these questions in your own business. Their employees did not deliver the experience we were expecting. How do you ensure that doesn't happen to you?

You work backward. Most people create a training system and see what happens. But I want you to start with your pillars and your desired customer experience and work backward, essentially reverse engineering your training. If you don't have your systems systemized and documented, this can be very difficult. However, I have a program called Employee Launch, and I'll teach you some lessons from it shortly. What we're really talking about here is training situational management to create that stellar customer experience every single day. This is hard and takes time to develop. Like everything, it's a mindset. But there are some helpful things we can do to ensure we end up with the right employee avatar and train to the result we want.

PREDICTIVE INTERVIEWING

Training starts from day one, in the interview. With the three pillars, you've decided what your employee avatar is and what experience you're trying to create for the customer. The training program I created is called Employee Launch, and my oldest daughter, Brianna, helped me build it and runs it for me. It's a software program that works in any position in any business and builds out a customized training progression for them.

When we are hired by companies, we usually start with the best employee in a position and analyze what made that person so successful. Then we build out a training pipeline that includes all the tasks that a person needs to master to go from a complete novice to the best in their position in the shortest amount of time. It saves companies so much money to have employees up and running as quickly as possible, and it makes the employee feel properly equipped and confident in their job. We first developed this for my Italian restaurant, and we have full training programs for management all the way down to dishwashers and servers. It's too detailed to explain in just one chapter, but I'll get into some lessons from the program. We use something called predictive interviewing, which allows us to accurately predict how successful someone will be in the job we're hiring for. The entire process of predictive interviewing is outside the scope of this book, though you can find more information here:

The basic steps are outlined next.

STEP 1: LOOK FOR EXACT EXPERIENCE

Ideally, you're looking for a candidate who has experience in exactly what they'll be doing for you. We're a full-service Italian restaurant, so I want someone who has experience in a full dining room and not just at a pickup restaurant. That wouldn't rule somebody out, but I'll know going into it that they require more training, and in my program I'd start them at a lower tier.

STEP 2: FIND AND/OR CREATE YOUR EMPLOYEE AVATAR

You can do the same thing we do at Employee Launch and look at your most successful employees in a position. Find your absolute best employee—this is your employee avatar. If you don't have an employee in this position yet, create an imaginary list of what you think would make for the perfect person. What makes them so successful? What experience do they have? That kind of objective information is important and will affect how much training is needed, which means more money spent for you. When Brianna goes in and does this for companies, she'll often notice a dissonance between what management says will make for the best employee in a position and the actual best employee in that position. They'll say, "Here is my employee avatar." But when the manager introduces Brianna to the highest-performing employee, they don't match up well. That can be tricky because someone is wrong. Either that employee isn't as great as the manager thinks, or the manager doesn't have a good vision for the employee avatar. Part of what we do is optimize that and help companies overcome the challenges of making those two more aligned.

STEP 3: UNDERSTAND THE
SKILL LEVEL REQUIRED

You need to understand if the position you're hiring for is a highly skilled position or an entry-level employee who might be brand new to the workforce. The training requirements for those jobs will be very different. What are the needs of your business? Since you've been through systemizing your systems and delegation, you should have a good idea of this already. In my businesses and in Employee Launch, we use a level system to evaluate employees from 1 to 10. Throughout the interview, I ask questions that align with each of these levels and use that to decide how much training they'll need. Levels 1 and 2 are pretty basic questions. For example, Can you use a nail gun? Do you know how to mix concrete? Levels 3 and 4 get more in depth: Can you build a set of stairs or read a blueprint? If a potential hire starts to stumble around the level 3 questions, I know they'll likely come in as a level 2 employee. Try not to hire from a place of desperation but from wisdom, especially if you need to hire some of those more skilled workers. So many business owners decide to become entrepreneurs and then realize they are drowning and need help right now. Anybody with a pulse. That's not a good decision and almost always leads to hiring the wrong person. Hire from a place of maturity and preparation.

Remember, this kind of objective experience is not everything. It's just step one, and it's easier to analyze and find than someone who fits the company culture. The subjective is critically important as well. *Who, not how* is a popular phrase and book in business because it's true. You may have to train someone to learn skills, but training mindset and personality is much harder. Does this person have the kind of personality that helps create the culture I'm looking for in my company? To see how self-aware they are, I like to ask questions about times when they were criticized by a manager in the past and the ways they need to improve. If they answer, "I've never been criticized," then I know they are likely deluded and won't take feedback well. I also like to ask people what their closet looks like. Some of the positions I hire for require an extremely organized person, and their closet can be a great representation of this. Or maybe they're more creative, like a marketing person, and their closet is a mess. Are they analytical? Are they free spirits? If the employee is mostly going to be working by themselves unboxing things, personality might not matter as much, but they need to be diligent and efficient. This is a very dynamic process. It's a mix of experience-based and personality-based questions.

Let's say you've done your predictive interview and decided to hire someone. From there, you need a great onboarding process that makes sure your employee understands the standard operating procedures and tasks required. This goes back to systemizing your systems. Which you already have set up because you wouldn't have read this far if you didn't, right? To set this employee up for success, they need to understand the system behind every task as well as the thousands of whys attached to everything they do. Everything is geared toward them being able to understand and articulate the experience they're creating for the customer. After the interview you should know their actual skill level, how long it will take to train them, what it will cost, and their starting wage. Can you do that after an interview?

UPWARD MOBILITY AND FOLLOW-UP

Now it's time to train your employee. They need to understand the process and procedures of your company. Like I said, systems and training go hand in hand here. You need to have your systems identified to build an amazing training platform. If I assess in my predictive interview that this employee has a good amount of experience already in the job I've hired them for, they may come in as a level 3 employee. Often, for highly skilled positions, I know I can't hire anyone under a 3 because training someone from the ground up in that position will take too long and cost too much money. We take each employee through a training program so that they eventually become a certified employee, which means they're capable of operating in their position without supervision. That's a level 4.

Here's where most businesses stumble. They train their employee for six to twelve weeks and release them into the business. They're all trained now, right? They should be able to do this perfectly. That may be true. Maybe you hire a janitor and they can do that one job well, but what are you doing to invest in them? Remember, we're all about investing in people, not just hiring. Most of the time, if you ask someone who's been at a job for four or five years, "Tell me about your ongoing training process," they won't understand what you mean. "I was trained at the beginning," they'll say. That means there's no focus on upward mobility, and that's a huge problem.

We want to look at what it means for employees throughout the entire life cycle of their employment. If an employee stops learning, how can we expect excellence? This goes back to the follow-through piece of delegation, too. If an employee isn't executing well on a delegated task, there's a gap in your training program. Growth is essential. It should start on the first day and never stop. If an employee has been with me for two years and they're not learning, then I'm failing. If you don't want to learn, then you don't want to grow, and that's my philosophy in my company. I want to give employees the chance to own their own location someday. If they want that opportunity, we're here to teach them.

I'm an entrepreneur. I know there are seasonal and short-term positions, and that's okay. I know that's going to happen. High schoolers may leave and go to college, and people take new jobs. That's why I need effective training programs so that I can get them up and running as soon as possible and not spend a ton of time training new people every year with the inevitable turnover. That's inefficient and not good business practice. And then, if they want to stick around longer, there are always opportunities for upward mobility. I still expect that growth mindset from everyone and offer them the same chances to learn and improve.

So many of my employees tell me in our interview that they came here because there was a growth opportunity. People desperately want this. As a manager, are you creating those growth opportunities in your business for your people? Or are you just hiring them and leaving them alone? Showing people how to grow is the path to greatness for your brand. You need people on your team who want to scale with you, and that means constantly training excellence.

TRAINING NEVER ENDS

Let's recap. You've identified the right employee through the predictive interviewing process, hired someone, and determined their skill level. Now, based on their level, you know their pay rate and an estimated time to train. A level 3 cook may take three weeks to train and start at thirteen dollars an hour. Once they've been through the training and are a certified employee, capable of doing their job well on their own, that's when I'm able to really start to make a difference. If a brand-new employee has been through four to six weeks of Employee Launch and is out there on the job, they may be working beside someone who has ten years of experience doing the same job. But I want that six-week employee to deliver the same experience to my customers as the ten-year employee. They're working with the same customers, and we want the same excellent experience. How do we do this? From a practical standpoint, it's about testing and communication. Training creates consistency!

Most companies cannot possibly train every employee in the ten thousand scenarios that they're going to face on any given day. That ten-year employee has seen a lot of them, though. When I'm building manuals and training systems, I go right to that experienced employee and begin writing down all of the friction points they've experienced in their career. Calculate every mistake, because every problem is an opportunity, remember? It all comes back around. Ask your experienced and successful employees to tell you about the friction points they encounter and then train around those. Develop a training system around friction and turn problems into opportunities. This is how you train situational management. Your training program doesn't just involve how to sweep a floor or change a light bulb. It contains the situational wisdom of employees who have been doing the job for years and who have encountered almost every scenario you can imagine. That's how you close the gap between the six-week employee and the veteran. You take the friction points they have experienced and turn them into training.

Develop a training system around friction and turn problems into opportunities.

It's difficult to train a new employee. Creating upward mobility takes time. Like everything in business, you never arrive. You are never done. It is a constant process that you refine as you go. Until my employees become certified, they meet with managers daily to check on their progress and to evaluate the training system. Even after they're certified, we meet every two weeks to follow up and see how they're growing. The process is constantly being tweaked. The work is never done.

EVALUATE

How do you know if your training program is working? How do you know if your employees are able to execute? I may think everybody should be able to produce fifty widgets an hour, but maybe they're only producing thirty. As an owner, you can do fifty all day long. But that doesn't matter. I was once the greatest pizza maker, but after a few years, it didn't serve me well at all. It's not effective if only you can do it. Remember my real estate agent coaching client Mary, whose closing rate was phenomenal but the agents under her couldn't close nearly as well? It's a failure in training. Don't criticize people when they're not living up to what you think they should. Examine your training.

Often, when big corporations bring in a new CEO, they'll ask, "Where's the friction and where's the fat?" That's the first thing they do because improving the efficiency of a company is how you unleash its true potential. Identifying friction points like overscheduling and then removing them allows you to operate lean and mean. Once you cut out that friction point, people can see a clear path to growth. They love coming to work every day. They're not frustrated. You know your training system is working when people have this mindset and are able to create the result you're looking for.

ACTION STEPS

1. What is your employee avatar? Does it align with your three pillars?

2. Does your customer avatar match your employee avatar? If there's a difference here, where is the problem?

3. What does your interview process look like? Are you able to accurately predict how well someone will do in their position?

4. Have you systemized your training system? Reread chapter 3 again if you need to.

5. What does your follow-up system look like? How often are you meeting with employees?

6. Are you truly investing in your people? Be honest about this. Are you just hiring, or are you giving them the growth opportunities they want?

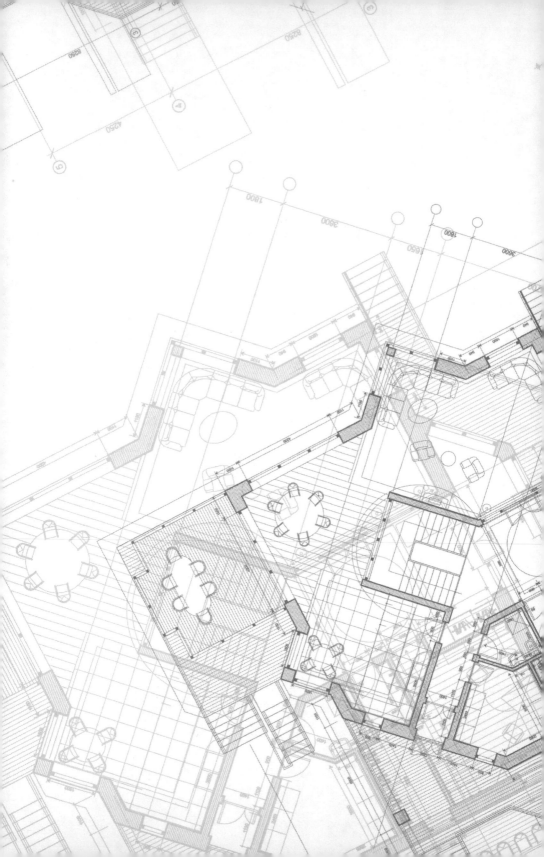

Branding with a Mission

GOALS ARE MEANT TO BE BROKEN.

Nick Halleran is a coaching client of mine, and he helps people build their own surfboards here in Virginia Beach. I've known him personally for years and have known his wife since she was a baby. He calls his business the Build-a-Bear of surf companies. Nick started the company a few years ago when he was only twenty because the build-your-own idea was the only unique angle he could come up with in a beach town full of surf shops. And I think it's brilliant.

I used to ask Nick all the time about his three pillars and his business plans when I'd see him at family events. We'd have a little whiskey and shoot some pool, and he'd listen to me bang on about business stuff. Eventually he got more and more interested and started asking questions. Our conversation soon turned to the name of his business, Dirtbag Surf Co. This came up in an earlier chapter, if you remember. I loved the name and still do. Sometimes I even ask Nick if he could find a way to work it back into his business somehow and sell it as a shirt or some paraphernalia. The name came about because he created the company at such a young age with what he felt was no trust or credibility in the industry. He was living in a nice part of town but in the tiniest little shack of a house with some friends because that's all he could afford. They were "dirtbags."

One day I explained to Nick that, as much as I loved the name, I thought it was really hurting his business. He'd been told this by others before but hadn't thought much about it. "Listen," I said, "if I'm scrolling through a list of surf shops, I have no idea what you really do. Making your own surfboard is your unique value proposition, but I can't tell that at all by your name. Not to mention you're a frequent activity for families, but I can't imagine bringing a young kid to a place with *dirtbag* in the name." Nick makes the most amazing surfboards on the East Coast, and he figured out how to create an experience business. When I send out a mailer advertising Ynot pizza, our pizza sales skyrocket, and the rest of our Italian menu drops off. Then, the very next month, I can send another mass mailer highlighting Ynot Italian, and our pasta crushes it while our pizza sales drop off. Marketing matters! What you highlight about your business matters. What you call yourself matters. Pretty soon Nick changed his name to Make and Ride Surf Exchange and redid all of his marketing to highlight that unique part of his business. It changed everything. It's hard to change a name you love, but it needs to mirror the experience you deliver. Use the billboard test. If you drive by a retail location at fifty miles per hour and quickly read a sign, you should know what they do. My reputation for changing business names lives on.

ARE YOU READY?

Training and marketing are where you're going to spend the bulk of your money, as I said before, so it's critically important that you know whether you're ready to market. None of the money you spend on marketing will be worth it if you don't know your three pillars, have systems, can delegate, and can train your employees to create the experience you're about to market to everyone. Is the foundation laid enough for you to seek out how to get those people through your doors?

If I were to go into a business and spend $100,000 on a huge marketing campaign to bring in one thousand new customers but I don't know what the brand's three pillars are, I will likely execute poorly and probably lose that $100,000. Those are the stakes we're talking about. And I'll likely lose a lot more than that because word of mouth is everything, and after that those one thousand people will not have good things to say about the brand. So when I talk about marketing, I mean knowing your brand, knowing your customer, having the right employees, and making sure you're prepared to win. This is how you achieve return on investment (ROI) marketing.

Not long ago I challenged my coaching client Sophie to up her billable hours from thirty a week to one hundred. She looked at me like I was crazy, but she loves to be challenged like that, so she was up for it. "You need to do some marketing," I said. "Get out there and call twenty urgent care centers to see if you can get more customers."

"But if I acquire those customers, I don't have the doctors to fill positions yet. It would overwhelm us," she said.

"Then first you need to call ten nurse practitioners and make sure you're ready to handle the volume. Get on the phone and get it done," I said. That's knowing your system. That's knowing what you can handle and making sure you're doing it in the right order. Training before marketing! Sometimes it's as simple as that. She's executing on a high level. She knows what she needs to do to up her billable hours, but first she's going to make sure her business is ready and her systems and procedures are perfect.

One of the biggest mistakes people make is that they market too fast. They're desperate for business, for a new customer, so they tell everybody and market before they're ready. When I first started my business, I put out a ton of flyers, and it resulted in an absolutely crazy night. The amount of business that came in was overwhelming. That

> ## One of the biggest mistakes people make is that they market too fast.

might sound like a dream to some of you. *Hundreds of new customers? Everyone wants that!* But I spent the entire night calling customers back and apologizing for messing up their order or not getting it out on time because I wasn't set up to handle it properly. I was so embarrassed. We recovered and have been in business a long time, but there are likely people who came that first night and didn't want to come back. Marketing won't solve your problems. It's the icing on the cake of an already perfected business strategy. Set your expectations. You may have to staff up a bit. Sometimes I need to increase staff before a big marketing push. I don't put the cost of those employees as a labor cost but as a marketing cost because they're necessary to execute. Don't spend any more money on marketing if you're not prepared. Instead, go back and work on the previous chapters first. Did you write down every single piece of every system? Did you list a thousand Ys for everything you do? Do you have a system for each one of those? That's the level of preparation I'm talking about here. If you haven't properly trained your employees and done everything in the first five chapters of this book, you're just throwing money in the trash if you're marketing.

I see this time and time again. People hire an agency for a big, fancy marketing campaign, and it fails. It doesn't produce the results, the ROI, that they're hoping for. So they try again. Maybe this time they go even bigger and spend even more money. And the same thing happens. But the truth is, it's not a failure of the agency or the campaign; it's because the person doesn't know their brand and customer well enough. They haven't invested enough time in figuring out who they are as a company. I'm an eager, aggressive entrepreneur, so I know this instinct. You want to get out there and get after it. But it's the wise entrepreneur who is patient and makes sure they're ready first. Do you know how to delegate? Do you have the right employees? Stop and think about all of these fundamentals before you move on.

LET THE THREE PILLARS GUIDE YOUR MARKETING

The three pillars really clarify your marketing. My rule of thumb when it comes to any kind of marketing—mailers, flyers, television, billboards, whatever—is that at least two of my pillars must be obvious in the marketing. If my marketing department sends me a static ad and it only represents one pillar, I throw it right back. The three pillars of Ynot Italian are family, quality, and community, so in a normal static ad, I will show a family sitting at a table in front of beautiful food. That has two of my three pillars. All that legwork we did in chapter 1 now pays off when we implement it in the marketing. The pictures and words you use in your marketing should instantly communicate your three pillars. People should be able to look at a snapshot and understand who you are and what differentiates you. So many businesses are about creative, funky ideas these days when clarity wins every time.

If you hire a big agency, you have to make sure that they understand your brand. I have found that they really appreciate it when I explain the three pillars and exactly what images and words I want to communicate. Once they even told me it was refreshing to work with someone who knows how they want to market. Like we mentioned in chapter 1, this is another place where you might want to gather some research from your customers. Ask them again what brought them in. What comes to mind when they think about your brand? What's important to them? Why do they care about your company? All of this is valuable information when it comes to marketing and can help give you some great ideas for communicating your pillars.

Letting the three pillars guide your marketing is the best way to increase your ROI.

A normal return on investment rate for a flyer or any solo mail piece is 1 percent. One percent! Why should we be happy with this? I'm convinced that this is only because people are not focused enough in their marketing. They don't know their brand well enough and they don't know their customers well enough. Understanding your customer avatar is important not only for creating experiences and products but also for marketing. What attracts them to you? Where do they hang out? Letting the three pillars guide your marketing is the best way to increase your ROI.

I cannot emphasize it enough—make sure you are truly ready when you start marketing. Stop and go back through the action steps of the previous five chapters. Have you accomplished those? Let them light a fire under you to build that great foundation so that when the droves of people come (and if you're marketing with the three pillars, they will!), you're ready to deliver on your promises and delight the hell out of them.

CREATE AN EXPERIENCE IN THEIR HEAD FIRST

Whenever I do any kind of marketing, I'm creating an experience in the mind of the customer before they even interact with my product. They can imagine themselves buying it or using it. If you're a hairdresser, maybe people can envision themselves relaxing in your chair and then ending up a better version of themselves with a great new haircut. With my construction company, I always try to get people to envision themselves in their gorgeous new home. So far in this book, you've heard me talk relentlessly about creating an experience, and marketing is where we really bring it to life. You want your customer to visualize it, see it, taste it. Get them excited about what they're about to experience.

Macy's is great at this, especially at Christmastime. They have beautiful pictures of women in red dresses and fancy shoes and perfumes that you feel like you can smell right through the page. Maybe the model has a man standing beside her, looking at her longingly. You can feel the romance and decide you need some of that perfume, too. So you go to the Macy's counter all happy and excited for your new product, and the employee doesn't even look at you, let alone smile. This is the execution and training piece, of course. She really brings down the experience. Maybe the perfume doesn't even smell as good as you thought it would because it's so tainted by this bad interaction. And at Christmastime! Those two experiences didn't match up. You got really excited and had a visual in your head but then your expectation wasn't met. This is why training before marketing is so important. Think of how that experience could have gone if the employee was trained properly. Think about how excited you would be after the sale if the experience had lived up to your expectation. You'd probably be shopping at Macy's again, that's for sure.

My daughter Victoria owns a jewelry company and spends a lot of money on marketing because she knows exactly who her customer is. She just did a huge photoshoot and hired a bunch of models. They're all beautiful and around a certain age. She sells a lot of her jewelry on Instagram and gets great feedback there from her customers. She knows what they're looking for and what they expect. Because she's not just selling jewelry, right? She's selling herself. She's selling an experience you have when you put on the jewelry. She's put the time in to understand her customer avatar and now can safely spend money on marketing because she knows she'll get that investment back.

Marketing also has a deeply emotional component. Think about what someone experiences when they interact with your marketing. Whether it's a testimonial or a photograph, it should paint a picture that makes people feel something. Even if I'm marketing something as boring as gutters, I'm not just going to slap a picture of gutters on there. Of course not! I'm going to put up a beautiful house that has those gutters, but they're so far away you can barely see them. What you mostly see is a beautiful house because that gets a much better reaction than gutters. It's implied that houses like this have these gutters. And everyone wants a beautiful house. I'd do the same thing as a real estate agent. Sure, I'll put up a picture of myself looking nice, but what I really want is a picture of myself inside a gorgeous house. Maybe even a waterfront property. As a construction person, when a real estate agent tells me that they want to sell nothing but million-dollar homes, I know exactly how their website should look in my head.

WHAT ARE YOU REALLY SELLING?

Gyms and weight loss programs are some of the best examples to look at when it comes to figuring out how to market to your client.

Think about gym commercials. Do they show a bunch of out-of-shape people? No! By and large, they show fit people because that's the experience their customer avatar wants. They want to be healthy and fit. Nutrisystem does something similar. They use an overweight person but only with a thin person next to them as a before and after. They're selling the transformation. They want their ideal client to imagine that could be them and how great it will feel when you look like that!

A fun counterexample to these is Planet Fitness. They intentionally market themselves as a gym in a judgment-free zone. But they're not really selling a gym membership. Think about this one. What are they really marketing? *Come be with your people. Safety. Community. Comfort.* It's still an experience they're creating for their customer, just a different one from most other gyms. Gold's Gym markets the experience of getting ripped and all of the benefits that brings to your life, and Planet Fitness focuses more on comfort and security. You don't have to be intimidated at the gym. Two different marketing techniques but the same idea. And, most importantly, they are set up to execute on this idea. I'm willing to bet that they train their employees with these exact experiences and customer avatars in mind. The Planet Fitness employees probably aren't jacked beefcakes; they look like normal people. And perhaps the Gold's Gym staff look more fit and even wear tank tops to show off their arms. This is your customer avatar and employee avatar working together. You need to think deeper about your marketing and figure out what experience or transformation you are really selling.

START WITH THE END IN MIND/ROI

Let's talk a little more granularly about ROI. Similar to the last chapter when we discussed reverse engineering the experience you want to create for your customer in your training, we start with the end in mind when it comes to marketing. Have a clear goal in mind. What result are you looking for? What would make this marketing campaign a success? Maybe you want fifty more customers a month. Whether you're doing your marketing yourself or hiring an agency, you need to have a standard. Tell your agency the exact result you're looking for. They usually hate this because it gives you something clear to measure them by. But it also provides accountability and forces them to deliver. I have hired and fired so many marketing agencies over the course of my career, all because I'm about ROI-first marketing. I hold them to that level and expect results. The way I'm able to know if I'm getting that return on my investment is that I track everything. There's not one piece of marketing that I do not monitor. I want to see what's working. I don't use a hope-and-pray strategy. I test and track to make sure it is worth my time and money. And if there's friction or breakdown in the process somewhere, I troubleshoot and turn that into an opportunity. Again, it is all about ROI-first marketing. Look at your company and determine whether there is one order type or product line that is struggling, develop a marketing plan specifically to accomplish the desired result, and then hold your marketing agency accountable. Do not be afraid to hire another marketing agency if you are not getting results. Marketing is too costly and is one of the biggest expenses in any company.

📐 ACTION STEPS

1. What are your three pillars?

2. Have you systemized your systems?

3. Have you delegated most of your daily tasks to focus on the high-level vision?

4. Is your training program perfected?

5. Do your employees know how to deliver an amazing customer experience?

6. Do you know your customer avatar?

7. All right, *now* you're ready to market. Get out there. Make calls. Print flyers. Email. Hire an agency. However you do it, with the foundation laid, you will succeed.

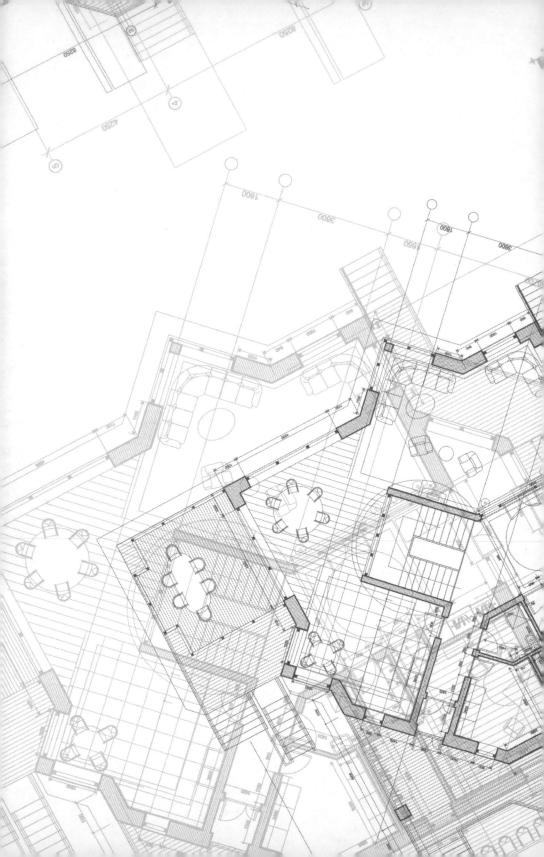

CHAPTER 7

Be an Experience Creator

QUALITY IS A STANDARD.

The Gaylord Opryland hotel is a famous and beautiful resort in Nashville, Tennessee. A woman named Christina stayed there regularly when she was in town for conferences. Each time she stayed there, she slept better than she ever did at home, all because of a unique alarm clock that played light music and had some noise settings she particularly liked. After staying there enough times, Christina decided she needed this alarm clock at her house. So she went on a hunt to find the exact model from Sharper Image, the manufacturer. But she couldn't find it anywhere. She even tweeted the hotel, and they told her their version wasn't available for the public because it was specially made, but they linked to a similar one.

Christina looked into it, but she was still disappointed. "This one doesn't have all the features I like about the ones in your hotel," she tweeted at them again. She decided to just let it go and enjoy the alarm clocks whenever she stayed there. Much to her delight, the next time she had a conference in Nashville and again stayed at the Gaylord Opryland, she found not one but two of those special clocks and a card with her name on it. The note read, "Christina, thank you for following us on Twitter. We hope you enjoy these spa sounds at home." Wow! What a way to make a customer for life, right? That meant everything to Christina and cost the hotel almost nothing. What incredible customer service. What a fabulous way to create an experience.

I know what you might be thinking when you first see this chapter: *Oh great! A chapter on customer service. How boring!* Am I right? *Another business book talking about customer service and how the customer is always right.* Even the words *customer service* either make people cringe or put them to sleep. Most people have a terrible idea of customer service. It reminds them of standing in line to return something only to be told they can't get their money back or waiting on hold for two hours and still not getting a solution to their problem. That's because the association with customer service is "someone has a problem" or "someone had a bad experience." It's hardly ever mentioned in a good way. That's why I don't use the term *customer service*. Honestly, I hate those words. If you've been paying attention and are beginning to think like an entrepreneur, you may even be able to guess what I'm going to say next. I don't believe in customer service. I believe in customer experience creation, in being an experience creator. Because here's the truth: anybody can provide service, but very few can create an experience (a good one, anyway).

When I was eight years old, my mom put me in a sombrero and a little shawl and had me sell Mexican pottery at her store. At the time, I just thought it was fun. But my parents knew exactly what they were doing. Putting a little Italian boy from Jersey in a Mexican sombrero created quite an experience for customers. It was entertaining and memorable. I know we've already talked a lot about the idea of creating an experience for your customer in this book. But I want you to really think deeply about it. It's easy to get into the mindset of wanting to be good at your job, creating a great product, making a lot of money, and scaling the business of your dreams. Those aren't bad goals; in fact, they're great! You need those goals. But the foundation of any business is the experience you create for the customer. Think about this: Every single person you interact with has an experience with you. What kind of experience will it be? Whether you're making pizza, building houses, pumping gas, selling candy, doing hair, cleaning floors, etc., every single person has an experience when they come into your store or use your product or service. Will you

> **But the foundation of any business is the experience you create for the customer.**

provide value? Will you make their day better or worse? Will you solve a problem they have? Will they think about you tomorrow? This is the power of a good experience. And that's all customer service really is.

It's not good enough to just mark off your checklist and hit your numbers. That's not what makes a great business, and it's not what makes people talk about your company and want to come back. This is a concept that is easy for some at the very top to forget because they are so far removed from interaction with the customer. When my friend John Legere took over T-Mobile years ago, they were going bankrupt. He once told me that when he came aboard, he focused only on one person—the person who sells phones at the front counter. It all happens right there. You can make the best phone in the world, but if your customers don't have a phenomenal experience with the product and with your employees, you're going to fail. Creating a unique, amazing customer experience is a lost art, but we're bringing it back. By the way, if you don't train those employees to articulate the benefits and sell it, then your marketing is all for nothing, and your systems won't work, either. This all happens together. I've made many mistakes in business. Many of the same ones I'm trying to help you avoid by reading this book. But one thing I did right was that my pursuit of the experience I was trying to create never wavered. Since day one in my restaurant business, I wanted a family atmosphere. I wanted to support sports teams, have high chairs, be a part of the neighborhood, watch my customers' kids grow up, and know people's first names. That has been my vision for thirty years, and I'm proud to say we nailed it. Because what I understood was 98.6 degrees. I was in the people business, not the restaurant business.

THE VALUE OF A CUSTOMER

Like everything else, customer service starts before anyone even walks in your door. It's the reason we began this book with the three pillars. You might be sick of me harping on this point, but it's that important. So much of my coaching is taking people all the way back to the beginning of their business, to the fundamentals of understanding their brand. Because everything determines the kind of service you will provide. Since you're reading this chapter, I trust you have that solid foundation now and know that the experience your customer has with you and your brand is a lot more than the thirty minutes or however long they actually spend purchasing your product. They're likely there because of some marketing you did that hopefully aligns with the experience they're about to have. You've trained your employees to deliver on that experience. You've hired and delegated so that you don't have to be the only one executing, and you were able to hand off tasks smoothly because you've systemized your systems. Right? Don't lie to yourself if this isn't true.

So, assuming everything in your business is aligned, let's talk about the value of a customer. What does the customer mean to you? You already have a customer avatar. You determined who your customer is and what problem you solve for them. But let's take it deeper and examine what the value is in each customer for you. The most quantifiable way to determine the value of a customer is to measure it. How much money do you make from each customer? What is your cost per acquisition? How much money did you spend marketing to them? What did it cost to train your employees to serve that customer? Knowing the answers to these questions gives you an exact ROI on each customer going forward. It gives you a fresh appreciation for exactly how important each customer is to your business and why investing in your customer is important. Side note: Not every customer is valuable if they're the wrong customer. What I mean is, if you are serving customers who do not fit your customer avatar, you are probably losing money in the long run. Even if a customer buys something, if they aren't aligned with your brand, they might not have a great experience with the product or come back. And in the worst-case scenario, they'll tell others about it, too. If you're targeting the wrong customers, the most likely scenario is you waste a ton of money and don't sell anything. Don't aim to create great service and experience for just any customer; focus on only the right customers.

But there's a more profound way to think about the value of a customer than just the monetary value they hold, as important as that is. Think back to your very first customer. The first person to buy your product or walk in the door and give you their hard-earned, almighty dollars for whatever you're selling. I mean the first real customer beyond your mom or spouse. What an amazing feeling, right? You were officially in business. It takes a lot for someone to get out their wallet and give you money. That's a huge moment for any business owner. What was the value of that customer to you? It's hard to quantify. Sure, maybe they gave you fifty dollars for your product, but it was about a lot more than that. You gave them something you're proud of. They were happy to receive it because they needed or wanted it. Maybe you talked to each other. Maybe they just interacted with the website you spent months perfecting. Either way, they had an experience. You gave them an experience. And they gave you money and the confidence to keep going. It's all about 98.6 degrees, remember? We're all in the people business, and one of the best business advantages is to keep that front of mind. What was the value of that first person who said, "Will you do my nails? Will you build my home? Will you make my birthday cake? Can you fix my problem?" Almost priceless, right?

There's a particular home improvement store that I won't name, but they have a reputation in my house for having some of the worst customer service I've ever experienced. I can't ever find anyone to help me in this place, and time after time my experience there is terrible. But sometimes I think back to the very first person who walked into that store to buy some wood. How do you think they were treated? Were they welcomed with open arms? Treated like royalty? Helped with absolutely anything they needed? Yeah, I'll bet you anything they were. The same goes for any big corporation these days. I wonder who the first person to ever buy a cup of coffee from Starbucks was. That was likely a life-changing experience, for both that customer and the founder and employees alike.

Treat every customer like they are your first. Value them like they are the lifeblood of your business, because they are.

This first-customer mentality is everything. This is what is so easy to forget when you're either working from your C-suite office or have been in business so long that you can't see the forest for the trees anymore. Treat every customer like they are your first. Value them like they are the lifeblood of your business, because they are. I could walk into any corporation today and change their perception of a customer immediately just by drilling down into this concept. One of my favorite questions to ask a founder is this: "Tell me about the first day you opened your business. Why did you start building bicycles?" Sometimes it takes a while for them to warm up and give me an answer beyond typical business lingo (gap in the market, good opportunity, etc.). None of that is wrong, but it's just not deep enough. Eventually, they almost always end up telling me about how they envisioned young kids riding their bikes down the road every day on the best and safest training wheels. The thought that someone would come in, buy a bike from them, and then have years full of fun rides is thrilling! It's dangerous for your business to let yourself get too far away from these feelings. This is what keeps you connected to your customer and allows you to keep creating that amazing experience for them.

Speaking of bikes, I remember the day I bought my daughter's first bike. We didn't have a ton of money yet, and I spent way too much on it. But it was for my baby, so it had to be the best. She's twenty-six now, and we still have that bike because I can't bring myself to get rid of it. Why? Because it's not about the bike! I'm a grown man and the CEO of multiple companies, and my daughters have been up and gone for years now, but I can't bring myself to get rid of a tiny tricycle for a two-year-old. That's the power of an experience. It's emotional and it's meaningful. All of this because someone sold me a bike over twenty-six years ago.

You have to think about this every day. You have to preach it. The only way you accomplish this in your company is to recreate this every day. Training is important, of course. We had a whole chapter on it, and

I built an SaaS product for it. So, yes, we have to train for this customer experience. But what I'm talking about here is more than that. It's a way of doing business. It's a mindset, a way of operating. You might have to work on it at first and do it consciously, but over time it should become second nature. This kind of thinking needs to happen instinctually in every part of your business. *What is the customer experience we're creating? What is the end result we're going for?* This is everything, and in a book full of my best wisdom, it might be the most important thing I have to share. I serve my first customer every day!

MEETING THE CUSTOMER'S EXPECTATIONS

Earlier in the book we talked about identifying your customer avatar. And a huge part of that process is thoroughly understanding the type of service that the customer is expecting. What is the outcome they're looking for? The way to provide outstanding—okay, I'll use the term here just so everyone knows what I mean—customer service is to simply meet or exceed the customer's experience expectation. I love investigating this in other businesses. Sometimes when I see a business do a ton of marketing and I develop an expectation of what the service will be like because of the brand they're putting out into the world, I go visit and see if it lines up with that promise they're making. Is what they're articulating actually what's happening in the business? This is why the show *Undercover Boss* is so fantastic, and I wish every upper-level management person could have the experience of going into their own business unnoticed and getting the real customer experience.

Outside of disguising yourself with wigs and makeup, a simpler way to get some feedback here is through blind customer surveys. I encourage all my coaching clients to do these as often as possible. They basically anonymously ask the customer how their service was and what they would improve. This data is gold. After you have this information, look at it and examine where something might be misaligned that created a suboptimal experience. Do you have the right training? Did their experience align with your marketing? Is there a customer service breakdown? Do you need to delegate more? Are the right people in the right positions? This kind of customer feedback isn't just about whether they received a satisfactory product or had a good experience. Take that information, good or bad, and apply it to every other chapter in this book. This is the secret to creating five-star service at a value price, if that's your business model. I have businesses that run the entire gamut of price, but in my restaurants I'm always striving to provide a Ritz Carlton experience at a Travelodge price, so to speak. Imagine if your experience at Travelodge could be the same as the Ritz Carlton. You'd be blown away, right? Creating that five-star service with a value proposition is a way to ensure that you win every time. That's how you go above and beyond the customer's expectations. Give them what they came for and more.

SET YOUR BUSINESS APART

For my real estate coaching client Mary, one of her agents does a very cool thing to create an experience for her home buyers. When she enters an empty home, she has everyone in the group sit on the floor like they're watching TV and imagine themselves in that space. Think what you want about asking people to sit on the floor, but this creates one hell of a fun, surprising experience, with the added bonus of talking about layout so that the customer can actually begin to envision it. When Mary told me about this, I asked how many of her agents do it, and she said just the top one. "Why haven't you made this standard?" I asked. "You need to get that agent to train that experience to everyone else. It's clearly working and it's unique." Actually, I teased her and said I would keep a pair of overalls in my car and be the best agent she ever hired.

"Whatever," she teased back. "You don't know anything about selling homes." Well, I've never been a real estate agent, but I do build custom homes, so I know a thing or two about marketing. I've also bought a lot of homes and done a lot of looking. But I don't have to know everything about real estate because I know about people and creating an amazing experience.

"I'd change into those overalls when we got to the house, go underneath to see what it's made of, check the plumbing, and see if the structure is all right. Those people are going to live there for the rest of their lives. I'm not just going to point out the obvious but make sure this is an amazing home in every way," I said. "Why do I do that? Who do you think they're going to buy from next time?" I asked her. She knew the answer. Not only would my hypothetical booming real estate business create trust with my customers but also it has the added bonus of the memorable experience of the real estate agent who changed into overalls and went into every nook and cranny under the house. "You better hope I don't become a real estate agent," I joked. She knew I was kidding, and she's one of the top real estate agents in the state, so competing with her would be no easy feat, but she took my point. This seemingly small thing could create lifelong customers, a meaningful experience, and ROI in the form of a great reputation that makes for more business. It shows that I care even more about their house than they do. I care about every single aspect of the experience as well as the final outcome, not just making the sale. That's the difference. If you focus on the customer experience, you will create a positive outcome.

I do this when I work with and coach architecture firms. I always tell them, "You don't have designers; you have experience creators."

What I want them to understand is that when they're drawing a home, someone will imagine themselves in those rooms, watching television, sitting at the counter, etc. I want the designers to see that, too. Think about the experience you're creating for the customer living in that house, not just the design you're drawing up at that moment. Which way is the house facing? If it's facing east, that might mean I want to put the living room on that side so that at night I have a beautiful sunset and the sun's not blasting me in the face in the kitchen while I'm having my morning coffee. This is the level of detail I'm talking about. Not just what looks or sounds best but what it actually means for the customer. Too often business owners do not put enough emphasis on this final touchpoint for the customer.

This laser focus on the customer experience is a serious competitive advantage for businesses. These days, convenience and technology are rapidly becoming the main aspects of customer experience. When I go into Shake Shack or Panera, most of the time I don't even have to talk to anyone. I order at a kiosk and pick up my food with zero human interaction. That's okay because they've set the expectation that you can get in and out quickly, and that's probably what that customer wants. Speed is everything. I'm a little old school and love human interaction, so this is not a pillar of my business and how we operate. I can't stand it. But I do understand that it works for plenty of businesses. If you see me out in the wild, though, and it comes up, I might get on my soapbox about the importance of human interaction with your customers.

One of the most critical ways to improve your customer's experience is to constantly be looking for and eliminating friction points. This is how you take your customer experience to the next level. We talked about this earlier in the book, because identifying friction is important for all aspects of your business. Look for any resistance or discontent in your customer service touchpoints. How do you make it less complicated? When you identify these friction points, that becomes a system you create to improve and eliminate them. Service does not take skill, but creating an experience does. I can have a ten-year-old child serve food, but a trained employee knows how to create an experience. The systems that you are constantly creating and improving are built to train this customer experience. This is also a great way for employees to set themselves apart in the workplace if they're looking for advancement or more opportunity. My experience creators are the most valuable employees I have, but this happens only if management is training them. Let's bring this full circle. You cannot expect an employee to create experiences if you have not defined the expected experience, trained it with your training system, delegated it to the right people, and marketed it to your ideal customer avatar to get them in the door. See what I mean? That marketing money is wasted if you aren't completely sure you can consistently deliver that positive customer experience. Now is the time to go back and read previous chapters if you need to or if you feel like your business is weak in one area. The whole point of spending so much time training your employees and explaining your Ys is so that we can get the customer experience we're looking for. It sounds trite, but everyone is having an experience. Your employees are having an experience of you as a boss and the culture of the company. That experience is translated to the customers in the form of systems, delegation, and training. Give your employees the tools to be experience creators. If you can take your lowest-level employee and train them to be a phenomenal experience creator, that will change your brand. That will make you unstoppable and allow you to scale as high as you want. But you have to do everything in between defining your three pillars and that final customer touchpoint really well. Let's focus on people and bring back the lost art of the customer experience.

🅐 ACTION STEPS

1. According to your customer avatar, what do you think is your customer's expectation of your brand experience?

2. Be honest with yourself: Do you think you're meeting that perceived expectation?

3. If you need to, conduct a customer survey and find out.

4. What is one extra thing you could start doing to take your customer experience to the next level?

5. What are some friction points in your customer experience pipeline?

6. What systems could you create to eliminate them?

7. Do your employees have a good understanding of the customer experience they're creating?

8. If not, how could you start training them?

9. Change the description of your employees. You can even steal my term: experience creators.

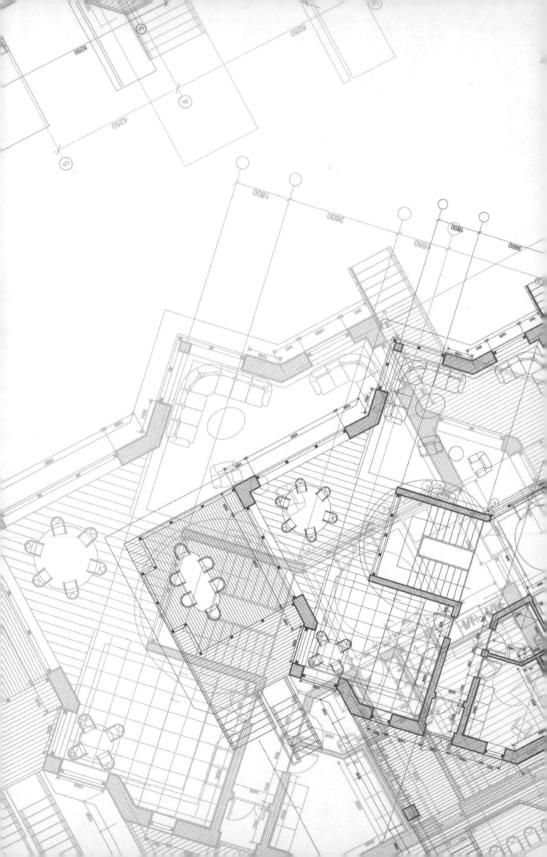

CHAPTER 8

Scaling

SCALING STARTS ON YOUR FIRST DAY!

Are you ready? This is what you've been waiting for, right? Scaling! You've dreamed of it, planned for it, and trained for it, and now it's finally time. Hold on. It *might* be time. As entrepreneurs, sometimes our minds are way ahead of our abilities. Remember those serial, overly ambitious entrepreneurs we talked about in chapter 3? That's me all the way. From the day I opened my business, I had franchising in mind, but it didn't happen for another twenty years. Sometimes we get too far ahead of ourselves. That's why we need a coach to keep us in check and make sure we're prepared for the next step. So are you ready to scale? This is kind of a trick question, because scaling technically starts from day one if you're building your business properly. What I mean here is that you've built a solid foundation, you have the pillars holding up your business, and you even have a few well-constructed floors. Are you ready to become a high-rise? How do you know? If you've read the last seven chapters and executed on everything, your mindset should be in line with your skill level. To scale, the technical processes in your business must be aligned with your mindset. When your wisdom and your ability come together, then you have the opportunity to really grow.

> **To scale, the technical processes in your business must be aligned with your mindset.**

As an entrepreneur, I grew too fast multiple times and almost lost my businesses. Remember the bakery I tried to open? I was emotional and overly ambitious. I didn't understand the drain it would have on my core business. I didn't understand what it meant to delegate and systemize. I thought I was invincible. But anyone can fail if they act rashly. To stick with our construction analogy, you may have only that first floor for many years. That's okay. Do it the right way, or you'll build that second floor before you're ready and lose both of them.

LET'S TALK ABOUT FAILURE (AGAIN)

You have to be ready for failure. I know failure isn't the happiest thing to talk about. I also know that we already discussed it earlier in the book. But it's all the more important to understand as we talk about scaling. When you exponentially grow your business, those micro failures that we talked about before become harder and harder to take. The stakes are higher. Every one of your decisions begins to have more money and impact attached to it. That's why building that entrepreneurial resilience with those micro failures early on in your business is crucial. As you scale, those calculated risks get bigger. That's why you need a mentor who has been there and made those decisions, too.

Eighteen percent of private sector businesses fail within the first year, and 50 percent fail within five years. Failure in business is real and painful. As a mentor, entrepreneur, and CEO, nothing breaks my heart more than seeing a business fail. That's somebody's dream that died. I see all the hours that went into it. The blood, sweat, and tears poured into it, only to have it close. It's terrible. One of my goals in my coaching and mentorship program is to ensure this never happens to my clients, because it is preventable. Businesses fail because they don't understand the fundamentals in this book. They think they can scale too early, but their building is constructed on a shaky foundation that comes crashing down sooner or later. That's why I keep driving home the point that you must nail down chapters 1 through 7 before you get here. It's not only because a lot of work went into this book and I want you to take it seriously, although that is true. It's because I'm trying to protect your business. Mistake avoidance is key. Don't move on until you're ready. This isn't about going slow; it's about being wise and ensuring your success in the long run. This is a sprint, not a marathon.

BUILD CONFIDENCE

Not too long ago, I went through a rough few months in my business. COVID-19 has taken the same toll on me that it has on others—labor shortage, new procedures, cash flow hits, etc. I was also involved in a few lawsuits that are typical for business but that are stressful nonetheless. It was hard. It felt like people were out to get me. I had to step back and recalibrate. First, I had to have compassion for those people making my life hard. They're people too, and I have no idea what's going on in their lives. I also had to lean on that entrepreneurial resilience I have built up over the last thirty years. The pandemic was interesting for me because the restaurants were shut down. My construction business was booming, but because of my systems and delegation, I didn't have to be as hands-on, and I had a lot of time to process. I started examining my systems, top-level employees, and marketing. I had never had this opportunity in business before, to slow down and really think through these ideas on a deeper level. It felt like when you go away on vacation and completely unplug and come back clearheaded. It was powerful for me. Remember, my motto is that every problem is an opportunity. On its face, COVID-19 was a huge problem. But I looked for the opportunity, and I found it.

First, I decided I needed to hire three new C-suite employees. We were supposed to franchise right before the pandemic hit and then that plan was put on the backburner. But I knew that everything would rebound and that we would eventually do it one day. Since I had time to slow down and think, I realized that my current C-suite wasn't right for franchising. They were mostly local people who didn't have the experience. I also knew that lots of big executives were losing their jobs during the pandemic and that the pool of talent who matched my vision was big. So I replaced three important people with others who better aligned with our next phase. A lot of people thought I was crazy for hiring during a pandemic. And hiring for huge, top-level positions no less. But I knew we'd recover, and I knew this was a big opportunity. I had been through recessions before, so I hedged my bets that everything would rebound. And it has. My restaurants are busy again, and we've since kicked up franchising again. After that, I dove into our pillar of community by feeding over two hundred thousand people in need during the height of the pandemic. I also started a new SaaS company that will revolutionize the restaurant industry through dynamic pricing, which is also blowing up. I believe I will look back at COVID-19 and say that it was the most pivotal time of my career.

But all of this was only possible because of the hard-won confidence I'd built up over the years. I knew I had the wisdom to make good decisions because I've made good and bad ones before and have learned from both. I've taken risks and failed and learned from those, too. This creates confidence—the kind that allows you to hire during a pandemic and continue scaling your business when others think you're crazy. You cannot scale without confidence.

Making big decisions and being responsible for everyone around you is hard. The bigger you get, the more obstacles and challenges you face. You have to step outside of that. Remember those two entrepreneurial traits: failing well and taking risks. Before you scale, you need these two traits ingrained in you, whether they were innate or learned. You cannot get overwhelmed and feel anxiety over every small thing. It will stunt your growth and strangle you. Tough times are inevitable. I've been through them. But you pick yourself up and keep going. Believe in yourself. If you've done the work and invested the hours necessary to understand these foundational concepts, then you are ready. And you can do this. Anxiety often comes from a lack of confidence, which comes from a lack of preparation. You build that confidence by nailing your systems, training, marketing, and customer service. That's what gives you the assurance that your business is ready and that you can handle the growth to come.

Once you realize that every failure is an opportunity for growth, now you're really doing something. Now you're really capable of scaling to incredible heights.

This confidence will allow you to take risks. And every time you take a risk, you're opening up the next threshold of risk. Do you know what I mean? I've founded over thirty businesses and made many, many mistakes. I can't even tell you how many mistakes I've made. I've taken many, many risks as well. And every time I took a risk, even if I failed, it gave me confidence to take another one. A bigger one. Because I survived. I learned something. It was an opportunity. Do you have that mindset? To scale, you must embrace this risk/failure way of thinking. Once you realize that every failure is an opportunity for growth, now you're really doing something. Now you're really capable of scaling to incredible heights.

YOU HAVE A NEW JOB

This is where entrepreneurs are born, right here in the scaling piece. If you're truly ready to scale, if you're confident in the seven previous chapters and you have a mentor in your life signing off, then you officially have a new job. Before you were a business owner, right? You were a technician, great and passionate about what you do. Now you want to double your business or open a new location or level up in some huge way. You want more. You're going to the next pinnacle. You're growing that high-rise all the way to the penthouse. That means you're officially in a different business. The mindset here is completely different. I bet you didn't think you were going to read this book and walk away with a whole different job, did you? In the first chapter, I introduced the concept of working on your business, not in it, and that's exactly what you need to do now. You've created the process and systemized it. You understand your customer, and you're delegating and training. Your marketing is on point. You are no longer a pizza maker, painter, real estate agent, builder, hairstylist, shop owner, plumber, or engineer. You are an entrepreneur, so think and act like one.

When I started my construction business, I began by remodeling bathrooms and kitchens. Then I wanted to grow and get into building entire homes. I went from being able to do a lot of the work myself to dealing with everyone from structural engineers and architects to painters, framers, and carpenters. I had to get rid of all the tools in my truck. I couldn't tile floors or knock out bathrooms anymore. I had become the general contractor. I had to be the one with the wisdom, process, and procedure to make everything and everyone work together. Typically, I only spend the first forty-five minutes of each day at a house to make sure everyone is following the proper processes and strategies. I've already trained everyone, so I don't have to babysit anyone. I just start everyone out on the right track and trust my systems.

My daughter who is currently scaling her jewelry business has big goals. She wants to be one of the largest fashion brands in the world. But she started out making the jewelry herself in college. She did braided jewelry, then as she got to know her customer avatar, she added gold-plated and wedding jewelry. Then she added clothing. She is always adding more products and leveling up. To do all of this, she has had to step back. Lucky for her, she didn't have to hire a mentor because she has me. She did hire an employee and is in the process of hiring more. She still does all of her own marketing and runs the TikTok and Instagram accounts. But she's really not selling jewelry anymore, right? She has a different job now, and it's something more. She's the face of the brand. She's what sets it apart. Recently she discovered someone who has somewhat ripped off her idea and is selling identical jewelry. It bothered her, but do you know what my reply was? "Victoria," I said, "do you know how many people make pizza in this town? Who cares. It's all about the bigger picture. Are you resonating with the right people? Are you creating a great experience?" This is the mindset of the entrepreneur. Your new job is to not get bogged down in these small ideas but to keep your eye on the big vision and to continue moving forward. Your mindset is what differentiates you.

There's a million of almost every kind of business. That's okay. You need to disrupt the marketplace. Create that unique experience every day and then you will scale your business.

CONSISTENCY IS KEY

All of this foundational work has led to this: creating consistency. The most important thing you must be able to do to scale is to remain consistent. People can argue about whether McDonald's makes good food, but what you can't deny is that it's consistent. They have systems and processes in place that ensure every single Big Mac you order from any McDonald's in the country is exactly the same. It's consistent and reliable. The same is true for Starbucks. Do you know how many people would get worked up if their caramel macchiato tasted different from Starbucks to Starbucks? There would be an uprising! Do you know how many people get upset when the cashier at Chick-fil-A forgets to say, "My pleasure"? They notice it because it's consistent from store to store. Like we talked about in chapter 7, they have an expectation that isn't being met. And that is the death of a business. These corporations aren't food businesses; they're systems businesses. They have an established brand and they function on systems. They have everything so perfected that they know exactly how long it takes to cook a burger down to the second.

Casinos are not in the money business; they're in the experience business. It just happens that money is a function of what they do. They're experts in creating a consistent, reliable experience for their customers every single time. No matter what business you're in, you can learn from and model this. As you scale, you have to be sure that every single piece of your business can remain stable and function well. The longer you have spent studying and perfecting the seven previous chapters, the more likely you are to succeed. This is about experience consistency. A telltale sign of an immature business is one that creates different experiences for customers every time they go in depending on the day, who's working, what product they're getting, etc. We covered expectations extensively up to this point for exactly this reason. Being able to reproduce those customer experiences and surpass expectations is critical.

HAVE A VISION

What is your long-term vision for your company? Have you thought about it? To scale, you must have a big vision. Often corporations bring in new CEOs for this very reason: to shake up the vision. My favorite hotel in Las Vegas did this recently, for the worse, I think. Previously it was the best service I've ever received in my life at a hotel. But then it changed CEOs and is completely different now. Why? Because it's two very different visions—two people with different priorities and perspectives. One valued certain systems and the other didn't. The second CEO was all about running a hotel that happens to be part of a casino. My opinion and preferences aside, they brought in a new vision. This is the same reason business owners hire partners or mentors. They need a new vision to scale to the next level. Fortune 500 companies and small business owners alike may struggle with one significant piece of their business (training, marketing, customer service) that gets in the way of scaling and creating that big vision. New CEOs can help here not only by creating a new vision for the company and diving deep into the three pillars but also by developing new ways to delegate, train, and systemize. Sometimes perfecting that one area is just what the business needs to scale better.

Somewhere in the pages of this book is the answer to a problem (opportunity) you have, I promise. Everybody's business has room for improvement. Identifying those elements will help you scale. Can you identify an area where you need growth? My goal for you is exponential but successful growth. My goal as your mentor is to save you seven to ten years of headaches by giving you the answers right here. You might feel ready to scale, but there is almost certainly an area in this book where you have room for growth. If you take the time and put the effort in, I promise that scaling your company will happen. This is a chapter about preparation. To reach your maximum potential, you must be prepared for that growth mentally and in every process in your business. I'll ask you one more time: Have you done everything? Have you thought about every single process and how it affects scaling? Are you making smart, educated decisions about your next steps?

I'm so excited you made it this far. Thank you for reading and sticking with me. My desire is for you to be able to scale your business to whatever level you want for the rest of your life. Thank you for trusting me to help get you there. Wherever you are on your journey, if you have a question, return to these pages. I know this is a chapter on scaling, but the truth is, you've been scaling all along. Since day one, you've had a vision and made progress. So you are scaling! Everything is scaling. Perfecting and improving your business every day is scaling. It's not necessarily a moment you get to but rather it's something you work on every day. What comes next is the ultimate scaling. What are your goals? Have you reached your biggest goals yet? Are you happy with where you are? Have you realized your dreams? If not, keep moving forward. Keep scaling, and keep growing. Return to the fundamentals, and keep your eyes on your vision. You can do this. It's been an honor walking you through *The Business Scaling Blueprint*. The next steps are up to you. Harness that fire inside you and never settle for less. Let's go!

ACTION STEPS

1. Are you ready to scale?

2. Can you identify an opportunity for growth in the previous seven chapters?

3. Do you have a business mentor in your life guiding you?

4. Do you feel prepared to take risks?

5. Do you feel prepared to fail?

6. Do you have the confidence necessary to grow?

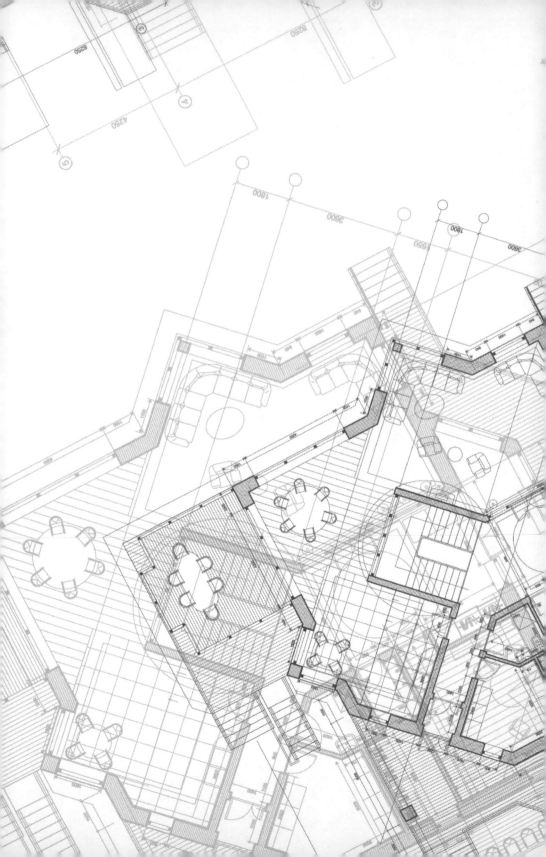

CONCLUSION

Congratulations, my friend. You made it through the entire book. I know it was challenging. I know that on every page I pushed you and made you think and even asked you to back up if you truly weren't ready to move forward. But we're done teaching now. Teaching is a huge part of what I do, but I'm a mentor first. And I've found that the message my clients need to hear most is this: You can do this. You're ready. You probably feel like you have so far to go because you have big dreams, and that's great. Everybody reading this has a huge desire to grow and has their eyes on the future. I do, too. You all are my people. But you already made it! You've already done it! You've been scaling since the day you opened your doors. You've made this huge leap and taken the risk. Every step gets you a little bit closer to your goals. You did something that 99 percent of people could never do: You started a business. You're officially an entrepreneur. That's no small feat. Stop and celebrate that! Acknowledge it and be proud.

It's a blessing to be a leader and to run a business. It's a big responsibility, but it's also a huge privilege to be a person of influence who serves and inspires others. I want you to be so proud of and grateful for everything you've done so far. When the going gets tough, try to be grateful. Remember this amazing business you've created and how blessed you are. Being an entrepreneur is the best job in the world. You get to serve people and create your own destiny. It was a privilege to do it together and to be part of your journey.

> **Being an entrepreneur is the best job in the world. You get to serve people and create your own destiny.**

I know that entrepreneurship feels like a lonely road. But you are not alone. You have me and so many others in your corner, cheering for you and walking this road together. I'm so proud of you for reading this book and for taking this journey. Never forget how far you've come. Let that fuel you to keep moving forward. You can do this. You have everything you need right here. And I'm here to support you however I can.

Keep going for your dreams and scaling as high as you want to go. The sky's the limit. You are amazing, and you only have one life, so go for it!

ACKNOWLEDGMENTS

There are many people who helped me become the entrepreneur and the man I am today. I wrote this book to help entrepreneurs and CEOs win every day. That is what drove me. And without these people, my message would have never gotten out into the world.

Thank you to my wife, Cyndi, for pushing me to share my story and reminding me that the wisdom here will help others. Without you, none of this would be possible. As much as I love being an entrepreneur and CEO, my favorite role will always be father to Brianna, Victoria, and Alaina. You three grew up in a crazy house with a dad who worked long hours, always worrying whether I was a good father. But seeing you three grow up into incredible young women has been amazing. Watching you become entrepreneurs yourselves have been some of the proudest moments of my life.

Thank you to my father, Harry, and my mother, Cathy. Dad, your hard-nosed work ethic and Mom, your nurturing spirit, are huge parts of who I am today. You taught me how to work hard even when times are tough and be empathetic and compassionate to others. Even at a young age, when I didn't know any better, the entrepreneurial values you instilled in me gave me a massive advantage in life.

To my brother, Harry DiSilvestro—thanks for always supporting me and helping me grow Ynot Italian.

Papa Case, thanks for teaching me that "your satisfaction is our success." And thank you to my stepmother, Colleen, and stepfather, Steven, for surrounding me with entrepreneurial wisdom and always being there to guide me when I needed advice.

My earliest memories of wanting to be an entrepreneur always come back to my cousin Vick and his ice cream parlor. Watching him run that shop inspired me and planted the first seeds of starting my own business. I'll always be grateful for that.

Thanks to Chico for being so dedicated to the process, even when times got tough. Thanks to Kathy Ferebee for always believing in me financially. Kathy gave me loans to start my restaurant and construction businesses way back in the day when I didn't have much success yet. I've stuck with her for years because she always stuck with me.

To all the employees who have worked with me at my businesses throughout the years: thank you for inspiring me. You helped build this brand. Even when I was crazy, you stuck by me and trusted the process. Thank you for listening and believing in me and this mission.

And last but not least, thank you to everyone I have coached throughout the years. It is because of you that I was inspired to take this message all over the world.